INKBLOT MOON

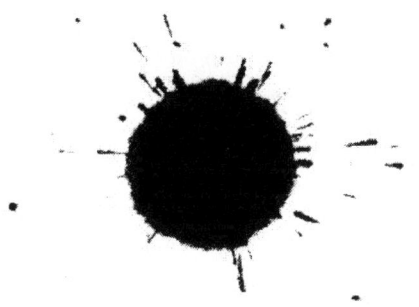

The Complete Quantum Poetry

Marcus Demetrius Link

Inkblot Moon: The Complete Quantum Poetry
© 2024 by Marcus Demetrius Link
Some rights reserved.

The author has asserted his moral rights to be identified as the author of this work.

The author has licensed the work under the Creative Commons Attribution-NonCommercial-ShareAlike 4.0 International. To view a copy of this license, visit https://creativecommons.org/licenses/by-nc-sa/4.0/.

Layout and design by the author. Typeset using *Garamond* and *zai Olivetti-Underwood Studio 21 Typewriter*.

A Terranomica *Keystones* Publication, books for inner transformation and outer regeneration published independently in the UK by Terranomica Ltd, Brimbles, Ashburton, Devon TQ13 7HU.

Visit www.terranomica.com and www.foolsjourney.me for more.

First Edition
ISBN (hardback): 9798333668288

"Who looks outside dreams.
Who looks inside wakes." C. G. Jung

"Seek not to follow
In the footsteps of the wise.
Seek what they sought." Basho

"Asmenos ek thanatoio.
(Glad to have escaped from death.)" Homer

Dedicated to the Future Pilgrim and the Children of Tomorrow, and especially to Leon and Luca, TT and Izee, Lotti, Julius and Elfie, Linus, Justus and Pauline.

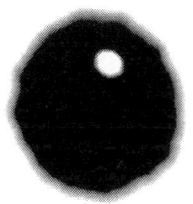

CONTENTS

FOREWORDS

By Richard Wain 2
By Claudius van Wyk 6

VOLUME III
THE LIGHT FROM BEYOND THE INKBLOT

Wyrd Awakening - Part I:
The Boy Receives an Invitation 16

Wyrd Awakening - Part II:
In the Deep Structure of Infolded Wholeness 28

Wyrd Awakening - Part III:
My Fall into this Small Bundle of Self 34

Wyrd Awakening - Part IV:
This One Outer Keystone 40

The Sacred Oath of the Quantum Poet 45

Two Rivers on Dartmoor 56

The Explainer Bird 61

VOLUME II
QUANTICLES OF EMERGEBNCE

Moulting... 68

The Little Man Dancing in My Heart........................ 74

Bits and Pieces of the Soul....................................... 77

Promise of a Man 80

Descending into Myself.. 82

I Am Your Vessel, Not Your Captain......................... 91

Out of the World, Into its Middle 93

VOLUME I
POEMS FROM THE GLOBAL VILLAGE

The Death of the Human Situation......................... 96

All the Riches I Inherited.. 98

By the Grace of My True Yearning,
For What I Am It Has No Price 100

My Gallows Star 108

EPILOGUE
AN EXQUSITELY
TERRIFYINGLY JOLT

On the Origin and Meaning of Quantum Poetry.......... 112

ON COPYRIGHT

You and I, dear reader, we meet in the deep centre beyond the eclipse of the inkblot moon, and everything you find in these pages: it is already yours.

Sometimes, writing is like a stepladder into the inwardness of myself. Other times, it feels as though I am being written into being by a poem maybe even over a few decades. The air flies the bird. The water swims the fish. The path walks the pilgrim. The poem writes the poet.

This is the experience of being true to my nature which involves these words that arise in the well within. They want to be heard and felt and sounded and shaped. It is a phenomenon which I understand as ancients like Hesiod and Ovid did and moderns like Kingsley and Hughes do: they are a gift like my breath from within and beyond myself to be treated with care.

By extension, my word is my gift to you, and I invite you to think and feel of it as you must and may and to use it as you wish – with due acknowledgment.

ACKNOWLEDGMENTS

My gratitude to all those who recognised, nurtured and encouraged this sing-song voice which rises within me.

You know who you are and what you have done. I hope you will find joy and satisfaction in seeing that I have done it here as it must be done by one who is blessed and cursed by the nature of this voice and the dual allegiance to and dual citizenship in the inner and outer worlds which follow from it.

FOREWORDS

FOREWORDS

What It Is to Be Part of an Infinite Interconnectedness

A Foreword by Richard Wain,
poet and author of Beyond the Brink is the Beginning

Yealmpton, Devon, UK, July 2024

There are many kinds of celebration. We join the threads of life, greet the rising and setting of the sun, mark and remark each rotation of the earth, we smile, we dance, we share stories, and it is in these moments, often, that we feel most alive.

It was many years ago at one such celebration that I first encountered the glowing ember of intellect and imagination who would one day jump over the *Inkblot Moon* and fill these pages with light.

A tall, striking man, all cheekbones and fierce intensity, Marcus made a lasting first impression. He attended my wedding as a plus one and his immediate impact on myself and my beautiful wife Susanna was to stand out, both as a person who we did not recognise and also a person who we were inexplicably drawn to. There has been a splendid poetry to the winding rhythms of our lives since that first meeting. We have shared in innumerable celebrations, moving closer, drifting further, but always in orbit, like moons compassionately guiding the tide of each other's world.

A quarter of a century passes, much like a thousand years, in the blink of an eye. The man that walked into my wedding, already a poet, has wrestled with many forms of entanglement in attaining his Quantum form. He has participated in business, in education, in family and in friendship with that same fierce curiosity and determination that shone through on the day that we met.

Though every conversation with Marcus is memorable, I remember one particularly intense exchange during which he laid out his plans for an extraordinary regenerative project called New Foundation Farms. The seed of this idea seemed wildly ambitious and romantic to me, and I watched on from afar as the seed germinated into the sapling of a radically natural business, a source of so much potential that I often felt the pull of its gravity on my thoughts. What if we acted as a beneficial keystone species on Earth? What if we could embrace our role as custodians of a thriving planet and let the abundance of life nurture us in return? As well as inspiring my own poetry, these questions guided the New Foundations Farm project as it became a solid reality, a farm, nestled in the beautiful rolling green hills, between the wilds of Dartmoor and the rugged cliffs and windswept beaches of the South Devon coast.

And so, on the night of the summer solstice, in 2024, another celebration took place. We gathered outside a whitewashed farmhouse on a still, clear evening, a group of fifty or so supporters of the New Foundations Farm project, connected by joy and excitement for the farm's inauguration. As dusk began to fall, we were led at first along a farm track and then through fields of long grass, weaving upwards to the highest point at which a circle of hay bales had been arranged. We sat facing each other on those bales, the sun setting, the full moon rising. We sat and we smiled, shared the warm, bitter delight of cacao, listened to the music of this wild place and watched the magical painted sky, brushed amber and green by the last of the light.

There followed a blessing. A ceremony of solemn beauty that I will never forget. It was presided over by Sujith Ravindran, a man of astonishing presence and warmth who made the same instant impact on me as Marcus had done all those years before. I cannot remember his words or his actions that night, but I can remember the pin sharp feeling of oneness and connection that he created. I can remember the sense that everything could be and perhaps already was. I can remember the sense that, whatever happens next, we have the individual and collective power to face it. In Marcus's life and his poetry, he embodies this spirit. The book is just more evidence of his capacity to see what is

INKBLOT MOON: THE COMPLETE QUANTUM POETRY

worth celebrating and to strike out towards it with energy, with passion and with courage.

And now it is time to celebrate with Marcus once more. This time we mark the rising of the *Inkblot Moon*, the expression of what it is to be part of an infinite interconnectedness. There is so much to celebrate in these pages, so many shared threads from which we might weave a new relationship with ourselves, with the web of life and with all that surely follows. I will leave you with these words from *The Sacred Oath of the Quantum Poet* on page 45:

Like this inkblot on my page
contains all the patterns of the world,
This journeywork of moonlight
Transforms me and my joy
And my sorrow
Into a tiny seed
Of another tomorrow.

FOREWORDS

A Welcome Gift on Our Journey of Human Becoming

A Foreword by Claudius van Wyk,
change agent and holistic thinker, founder of the Holos Earth Project

Lanjaron, Spain, July 2024

There is a growing awareness that many of the existential challenges of the world are a result of our prevailing Western paradigm of thinking. Especially with so-called rational modernism, Western culture reduced existence to quantifiable material phenomena.

In the poetry of *Inkblot Moon* and its essay-epilogue, Marcus' revealing personal testimony expands eloquently on the myopia of this perception from his own first-person experience and goes on to present a radically transformed perspective to the prevailing frame.

In his testimony and poems, qualities of experience – feelings, insights, beliefs– are revealed as being of fundamentally greater significance than mere epiphenomena of physically measurable processes.

Much of my life and work has been influenced by Jan Christian Smuts' articulation of holism. It is now nearly a century since he introduced the concept of *holism* into the world as a way to take issue with the materialist perspective. Ultimately, his holistic perspective focused on emphasising the greater depth of human *Personality*. It is a term which has been appropriated in many forms of organisational application, but its deeper spiritual essence has hardly been grasped. Marcus' evocative verse serves to open a window which allows in the refreshing air of an enspiriting sense of a deeper reality.

How might *Holism* connect to *Personality*?

Cautioning against its more superficial interpretation by, for example, complexity thinker Edgar Morin criticises as "amounting to everything being thrown together in a plastic bag,"[i] psychologist Guy du Plessis[ii] emphasises that Smuts used the word holism in a metaphysical sense.

Where holism is often seen as restricted to the manifest material domain – a collection of physical parts more than their sum –, holism as conceived by Smuts is actually intended to express something that is even more than a psychic function: it is a creative participation in which we may become whole-makers. And so, quoting Smuts, du Plessis stresses that holism is an ontologically infolded principle-and-process inherent in nature:

"The great whole may be the ultimate terminus, but it is not the line which we are following. It is the *small natural centres of wholeness which we are going to study and the principle of which they are an expression.*"[iiii] (my italics)

The functional view of holism sees it as the whole being a function of emergence arising from its complex interactions. But the metaphysical perspective regards the whole as an active agent in its own manifestation. In other words, the whole is already in there *in potentia* and is involved in a *process of becoming*. It was in this way that Smuts differentiated his perspective on holism from, for example, A. N. Whitehead's thinking on process and emergence. And, it is this metaphysical perspective which also differentiates holism from complexity theory.

This agency of the whole itself which is identified by the metaphysical perspective is exemplified over and over again in Marcus' revealing personal testimony. His work is a personal exploration of one such a *small, natural centre of wholeness* and, at the same time, his becoming into greater wholeness is the principle of which he is an expression. And so, with Smuts, he recognises his relevance in the whole. His exploration of his own wholeness and the emergence of wholeness are "entangled" in the same creational act of becoming.

Following Smuts' view that the path to holistic personality is through *inwardness*, Marcus references Daniel Schmachtenberger, implicitly, and E. F. Schumacher, explicitly, both who emphasise the missing *vertical dimension*. Poetry, thus, provides access to such inwardness which is simply another way of expressing the vertical. When we go higher on the vertical, we don't go upwards. We go inwards.

In his essay-epilogue, Marcus makes the point that in response to "a soul wanting to be born" on the journey of inwardness, holism is about outer openness and inner coherence. In this regard, he also quotes the Jung-Pauli emphasis on the non-duality of psyche and matter in advocating embodied human agency.

In *The Divine Comedy*, it is Virgil who accompanies Dante through the *inferno*, and Virgil himself had previously written in Aeneid: "The spirit within nourishes, and the mind, diffused throughout all the members, sways the mass and mingles with the whole frame."[iv] A description of a vital force that animates and sustains the body, permeating every part of it. The passage occurs during Aeneas's journey to the underworld, where he learns about the nature of life, the soul, and the afterlife.

Against the hubris of scientific arrogance, Marcus quotes Tyson Yunkaporta when he says that Western culture is still adolescent. But Marcus also points out that McGilchrist' right-brain state of awareness, when informing left-brain logic, may still offer a *third way*, a redemption of a gift buried inside Western culture. We might still be able to find our way forward (rather than backward) on the path to a more ethical future, one where embodied experience, enabled by heightened sensitivity to feelings, responds to nature's natural patterns, without losing the possibility of fine differentiation offered by the left-hemisphere of our brains.

In *Inkblot Moon*, the lyrical, and sometimes visceral quality of his writing, often has the feeling of an ode. Addressing both the left and right hemispheres of the brain, the description of his emerging insights in what surely is his *confessio fidei* – the articulation of his faith – is deeply intellectual whilst his vivid poetry speaks emotionally.

For example, his *Two Rivers of Dartmoor* (page 56) sensitively integrates both a physical and meta-physical intimacy. Whilst it talks to Bertrand Russell's *widening stream* (How to Grow Old) and Eugene Marais' *Deep River*, it does so with an embodied physicality.

Jan Smuts, addressing students shortly after publishing his seminal *Holism and Evolution* in 1926, focused on his deep inquiry into holistic Personality. For example, he said of his research into the German scholar, poet, novelist, and playwright Johann Wolfgang von Goethe and the US American poet Walt Whitman that there was much more to them than was revealed in their works.

Marcus' book, especially through the poetry, provides entrance into the depth of his emergent being of which his public activities and utterances merely provide a glimpse.

I have known him and collaborated with him on the Holos Earth Project for many years, and I take great pleasure in witnessing his evolution as a thinker and writer. I am especially pleased that through this publication (and hopefully more to come) his voice can reach and inspire a wider audience.

In short, *Inkblot Moon* is an emotionally deeply satisfying and intellectually stimulating masterpiece. It reveals the essence of the visionary, reverent and humble spirit that moves the poet that is Marcus Link. It is a welcome gift on our journey of human becoming.

FOREWORDS

THE LIGHT
FROM BEYOND
THE INKBLOT

Quantum Poetry

Vol. III

WYRD AWAKENING

A Long Poem in Four Parts

Conceived while travelling on
the west coast of Norway in
August 2023. Completed in
Ashburton, Devon in February
2024 on my return from India.

WYRD AWAKENING
- PART I -

The Boy Receives an Invitation

Once upon a time,
as a mere boy of eight,
I was sent an invitation
which, though always open,
I did not so readily receive.

I was a mere child then,
when I read a magically infolded story
about a child reading a story
about a child-hero of the native kind
who was at home on horseback
in the prairie with the buffalo.

He found himself tasked
by the healer Chiron
with the quest to find a cure
for what it was that
ailed the Childlike Empress
who had fallen ill in the Ivory Tower.

The illness which had befallen her
– and her entire realm –

was to have been forgotten
not just in name
but in reality and in being also.

Her world of imagination
became the Nameless Realm,
and she the Nameless One.
She was fading
as her realm was crumbling,

Light turned to darkness,
images turned to fragments;
all at the hands of
the great Nothing
While the questing hero-child Atreyu
lost first his horse to the fens,

Which overcome all things
with suffocating sadness,
and, then, from around his neck,
he lost to the deepest waters
of the deepest sea,
Auryn, his protective amulet,

Fashioned from two infolded serpents
biting each other's tails,
which also had inscribed upon it
that same eternal truth of consciousness
in Gothic script
just in case it was forgotten:

Do What Thou Willst.

In spite of the seeming
hopelessness of it all,
with the help
of the luck dragon Falcor,
Atreyu did find
that indeed there is an edge

to his realm where it reaches
not only into the life
of the reading boy
but into my day-to-day;
a most important infolded
and fertile boundary,

a juncture which really is a path,
at which the sheer force of that
which always pushes up from below
to form the mandala of a flower
from deepest lightless root,

moved the hero just as all was lost
- or so it seemed -,
to still give such insight
to the Nameless One,
that she must speak to
the boy-child reading
this infolded cosmic drama
in yonder realm,

one story layer back,
which is as magical to those
who inhabit the imagination

as they are to us.
She must tell the boy
that her sickness
was her namelessness,

and that her cure
was a name spoken
by an earthly child,
and that it was his gift
to make it so that
she might be un-forgotten
and re-remembered
from deepest bone,
though not even yet known
or before encountered.

The reading boy
within the story,
he hesitated
in his sense of unworthiness
and in his hesitation
the Realm withered
to but Nameless Empress
and grain of sand.

And all this took place
in his own withered soul
when he finally
called out *Moonchild*
into the night sky
and into his own

being and soul
as his chosen name for her.

And what saved her
saved him and saved both
his realms, inner and outer,
and reached beyond
the realm and page into me
as thunderbolt of terrifying awe
made of equal parts
exquisite fright and
terrible rapture
so that I would never forget,
and I did not.

Four decades
I have been questing
to understand
what happened then,
that I knew something
to be true
but could not find word
to say or outer recognition
to know of my
inward disposition.

Yet, so it always is
And always has been:

The old King has three Sons:
one simple, two golden ones.
The golden children are lost
to the ways of the light,
one left and one right,
and only the Simpleton
finds his way through
the darkness to three
Witches and one Princess.

They have twins
and once more
we have four.

The Four becomes the Three,
then Two and then One,

The Four as the One
finds rejuvenation in
the Kingdom Beneath the Sun.

There's a dance of such
triads and quaternions,
of such constellations
breathing in story and song
which enumerate
in archetypal sequence
a living web around
the totem of Self which is,
because of the archetypes,
though always vague and hazy,
and yet also gives rise to them.

Wholeness is always of
aspects and parts and
also its own thing too.
And no one thing
is in turn itself ever
wholly One and bleeds
at its edges into the next
in the dance which
is whole making and
in which the Self is
invoked and arises
out of the deepest centre,
a thing both of
the most distant past
and always only in the future,

yet ever present,
as the whole which
transcends and induces
the parts in their
perpetual motion:

Self is spun as it were
from the dancing and breathing
which are the fibres of its manifold
which interlinks life
with life through
a more-making death,
always itself and
always part of another
as it in turn gives rise

to the roots of
yet more nested wholeness
and layer upon layer of being.

And so it is
with voiceless music
of the archetone
and its ethereal
chordal floods,
its gritty grating staccatos,
its pattern of sound
inside and beyond
the pattern of word.

Its weave is always
in relation and between
its relations becomes itself.

It might take
the cry of the eagle
and string it with violin

to the highest note
in the final Ciaccona
of Bach's Second Partita
to weave out of the
too early death
of his beloved wife
a musical tombeau
and fractal sound womb
in which not only she

is resurrected, but life eternal
is traced in sound.

Though written only
for voiceless violin,
it gives birth to song
after song after song
if only my ears are
wide enough,
if only my soul
has such depth, to hear
the crisp dotted rhythms
telling of the
inevitability of death
from which we yet flee
in hasty 32nd-note runs
through unbearable times
of sorrow woven from
chromatic descent and
six-note progression and
strung out between
upper and lower voices
drawn from yet one instrument,

And always joy awaits
in the highest descant
above arpeggiated chords
inaudible yet implied
and alluded to,
the almost unmusterable patience,
the inevitability of joy

which now as bugle
sounds its fanfare
in bright triads still from violin
and the drumbeats drawn
from the wood beneath its strings
as a geometry of arpeggiated
four-voice chords
choreographs a dance of sorrow
and joy and delight
never yet encountered
but now known,
never before experienced
and now remembered,
induced from the wholeness
dormant in my bones,
inducted from the flow of my blood,
by the chords of this
rite-of-passage that is
bearing this gift.

Beyond what is countable
for my smaller mind,
beyond the ratio of relation,
audible in my soul
beyond my inner ear,
there reverberates a sound
formed from whole-number vibration.

The cosmos,
matter dark and bright,
living, dying and inanimate,

stars and suns and Earth,
mineral and animal,
human and plant,
beyond space and time,
beyond the tone in the tone,
and the partial fractal
of the root of the whole,
enumerated in number,
in story and song,
in the differentiated integration
of my mythopoetic matrix called soul,
archetone and -type and number
all once more become

One.

WYRD AWAKENING
- PART II -

In the Deep Structure
of Infolded Wholeness

If you must ask
what is the breathing dance of number,
of archetone and archetype
on the inside of things
beyond space and time,
I say look to the fields and forests,
look to the ocean floors,
look to the skies outside of you.

There are the fungal thousands,
and the microbial billions.
There are the buzzard,
the deer and the cuckoo,
the ant and the tree.

Archetypes of the community of land
whether above or below sea.
The swan song of the mayfly
in the winged cry of the oyster catcher.

The strands of seaweed
in the arms of Architeuthis,

the ancient squid,
woven together into patterns and flows
of the trophic cascade
of photosynthesizers,
and grazers,
of parasites and apex predators
and ecosystem engineers,
of daylight and
nighttime hunters,
of scavengers
and decomposers.

They are breathing and dancing
just like the archetypes in story
and the archetones in song,
enumerating in endless chains,
interlinked, hand in hand,
induced by and creating
the never still stillness,
the plurality of Oneness,
the fusion of the elements
into the totem of life.

The beaver takes stream and tree
to mesh wetland and
hundreds of species bloom
in this fabric which in turn
sits towards the valley
of the river basin
receiving the waters

from higher up the watershed
where they melt from snow caps,
trickle, drip and ooze
from naked stone
baking in the sun
and the wolf chases deer
across the mountain side.

In their footprints,
woodland and pasture
rise skyward and
a thousandfold of creatures
above and below
buzz, swirl and crow
and all drink of the water
which is stored with sunlight
transformed in the larder
of dark living soil crumb,
the skin of the body of Earth.

And again,
the stony bones
of the mountainside
ooze with the waters
which once were liquid oceans
and steam of clouds,
and then drops on a leaf,
then lubricant of the rhizosheath,
mixed with sun's rays into food
to pass on into grazers
above and below,

and on and on
until again as clouds
sun heat radiates
into the vastness of space
to cool the fire in the air
and the life in the earth.

I cannot tell where
biology
and physics
and chemistry
are one or the other
in this ecology.

I can only see
one deep structure
of infolded wholeness,
one whole into the other,
inducing and arising from
and into each other.

Liquid sunlight
mingling with mineral
passing from blade
to deer
to wolf
to scavenger
to decomposer
and back to plant root
and heat of sun which,
with the water vapour elevator,

returns to the breathing
outer edge of Earth
beyond its biosphere,
to be let go of into space
as infrared radiation
to complete the cycle
which sunlight had begun.

WYRD AWAKENING
- PART III -

My Fall into this
Small Bundle of Self

I can only
read the topmost
of these dizzying,
spinning patterned trails and traces,
these poems, songs and stories,
written into the hillsides,
and the wetlands,
the wooded pastures,
the kelp forests,
the cloud- and star-filled skies.

Little as I might be permitted
to read of the true depth
of these fractals,
I know them
to be more than accidental scribbles
on the uppermost parchment
of these lifescapes:
They are the very fabric
of this weave and mesh.

This is the story that lives.

This is the deep structure
of the Self
which breathes
braided time strands,

glistening with the sheen
of the archetype
and the archetone,
with psyche gleaming
inside of the skeleton of matter,
the maze which
knows not of higher and lower,
not of deeper and shallower,
which is everywhere
and knows us as distinct
and relevant,
and not as special
threads of its wholeness.

The edge is always infolded
back into its centre
and the centre
is the edge of the field.

The maze
in which I was found
when I finally looked
for my place and role
in the greater whole,
which in fulfilling it
ever more,
fills me out
ever more,
ever more myself,
it breathes,
as its energy flows

through me
in generative ways
across space,
across time.

Such a niche
of the deep structure
that is mine
right before me here
and under my feet
and inside of me
and in the far distant origins
and at the farthest edge of it all,
is mirrored
and reflected at all scales and levels,
to the horizon of myself
and beyond it.

My being ripples out,
it is more and more field
and less and less thing,
as I become more myself
and in turn leave behind traces
just as I am a shore
for other flotsam
which beaches
in my soul.

And these ripples
and traces
they touch upon others,

and in this way
I might be like sun
or black hole:
mine is both the generative way
of seeing others on their way
and also of using others
for my own designs,
not theirs,
and in such ways
that neither I nor they become
what we could have been
but we remain arrested,
remain locked,
and enmeshed,
not in chorus,
but in pain.

And novice though I am
at glimpsing it
from inside
and outside of me,
in my inner and
outer worlds,
I have caught sight
of my gods
on yonder side
of this deep structure
looking back at me,
and I have since
heard the whispers

of my calling
that was there
since before my beginning,
the calling
which launched me
as but a countable speck
from among their
infinite number
in the eternal
vast realm,
before my fall
into this small
but distinct bundle
of myself,
suffused with such
intensity of feeling
as I am and
because of which
I have grown from
templated,
generic man, into this
one more whole,
if more eccentric human being.

For others,
it will be different,
and I know not
and cannot know how.

WYRD AWAKENING
- PART IV -

This One Outer Keystone

In my case,
I fell
through the membrane
at the edge of psyche
and matter
and cleft open
the wound there
of my selfhood
which bleeds
with the time
I am made of
and which I exude,
like a starry pinprick
in the vast sky
must bleed
with the light
of its star.

I have been hurting since
because I am alive.

I must hurt
because I live.
It is one
and the same.

Yet, first
and for the longest time
I did not understand
that I had chosen this fall
to feel my way back
into the womb
seeing little as I might
on my way
but feeling
the deep structure
whence I came,
crawling back
from this surface place
and through that hurt
to even begin
to grasp
the possibility

that I have a place
in its midst
as a womb and
weaver myself

in the living
cosmic landscape loom
in which I am much less

and smaller by far
than any
of the starry pinpricks
across the night sky,
hardly a drop.

But no one
and nothing
has seen them
and felt them
and looked back at the gods
from this particular angle,
in this peculiar way.

That is why
I am here.
No one
has done it
quite as I have.

Through their patterns
above and below,
and I know it not like they,
and something
that is not mine
but because of me
and because of my existence
will come of it,
and that is my solitary
and lonesome privilege
to be this one small

and momentary
inner wholeness,
this one outer keystone,
over and through
which flow
the waters of life,
reflecting the light
of the gods
through my very own
tare in the world structure

which, though weak
and hardly visible,
shines yet so lively
with my own weave
and colour,
my own patina,
my own spark of light
embodied in this
aching blood and
these creaking bones.

The Sacred Oath of the Quantum Poet on His Inner Journey

Conceived during a pilgrimage along the river Narmada, Gujarat, India, January 2024. Completed in Ashburton, Devon between February & July 2024

The world,
it had a lively niggle,
it had an itch
to become yet more
than it already was.

It had a question
about the beauty
and wholeness of it all,
and out of this niggle,

itch and question,
it was out of them I grew.

It is only
a very small question
for everyone
has their own
and the whole world
is made up of them all.

It's just that it was
this one particular one
whence it came that I am.

So many philosophies
and beliefs abound
with the same things said
but dressed in different words
yet given mostly
as answers
and all at home
in some distant past.

In the Tao Te Ching
it says, "Only by being
lived by the Tao
can you be truly yourself."

So too the Christian
mystics speak of
"losing oneself
to find oneself."

So the Sufis say
with Rumi,
"I am not this hair,
I am not this skin,
I am the soul
that lives within."

And in the Bhagavad Gita,
Krishna explains
to Arjuna
that self-realisation
follows from
the surrender
to the divine
will of God.

The Buddhist
speaks of Anatta
beyond the impermanence
and interconnectedness
of all things, and
that we can attain it
through meditation
and through the way
we live.

The Lakota Sioux
refer to all their relations
in the larger-than-
human-community
which they call
Mitakuye Oyasin.

Both the stern and
unyielding Anglo-Saxon
and the stoic adventurous
Norse knew of the web
of wyrd that connected
them and their fate
to all that is
between everything.

The quantum scientists
speak of entanglement,
and that the wave
and the particle
are really just one,
and that its superposition
exists across
the unified whole

They all speak
of this invitation
that I too feel
inside of me.
I know it
in my bones.
I know it
because I am here.
I know it
because of that niggle
and itch of a question:

How can the splendour
of this Tree of Life
which is my home and yours
not be the lesser
because of me
but the more?

Like you,
Brothers and Sisters,
you have your own
and this simply is mine.
I have this question
which visits me
when I am as still
as still can be.

And I thank you
for this audience
that I might sing to you
of this question
which is also my oath
in which I pledge,
first of all, that
I may hear it,
and then that I may know
what it means.

You too
my Brothers and Sisters,
may find this sacred sound
and tone of a question

in your muscles,
your glands
and your bone.
You too
may step barefoot
on sand and stone
and cross the wilderness
in which before
you felt alone.

Breathe deep
into that underbelly
of the interconnectedness
of things where
your roots tickle
the fungal hyphae
well below your feet.

It only takes little
to join me. So
prepare yourself
if you will.
Close your eyes
and journey with me
as you breathe in
and breathe out.
And keep the pace
in this pilgrimage
of the becoming
of all of creation
by allowing ourselves

to be led by
the slowest of creatures
on our way
to the heart
of this thing.

So, breathe in,
breathe out.
Hold space.
Keep the pace.
It is time
for your Brother
to reveal his original face.

I was once
a burdened one
who yet awoke
to understand the spell
and curse he was under
as the outer shell
of an inner blessing.

I came to see
that in my shadow
there lies a gift
which makes it impossible
to just behold one song,
or one poem,
or one book,
or one sculpture,
or a flower, mushroom,

tree, fish,
or lamb or eagle
or any one thing
as only that one thing.

This Brother is one
who sees in everything
the trace and crystallisation,
the footstep,
the breeze in the woodland,
the ripples on the lake and ocean
of the forward movements,
the becoming,
the unfolding,
the unfurling,
the being born
of something
greater that cannot
be known now
as it is not yet
and yet we do know it
not in concrete fact
but in participation
and in feeling tone
when the electric current
from times gone by
into some distant future
runs through me right now.

Imagine you and I
we were not here

right now to conduct
this mighty thing
emerging amongst us.

It is that which fills me
with life when nothing else
will do.

And I am in service of that
which leaves this footstep,
this breeze and this ripple,
that which is that it is,
that which is the becoming
beyond that which already was and is.

I am the Quantum Poet
on my inner journey
where every syllable's a beat
and the beat's in my feet
and my pen is my staff
and the leap's in my heart
on my way to the root of the root
in the unity of life and beauty
and a momentary timeless state.

It may look like I'm walking
and it may look like I'm writing.
But if you look closer still
you'll see that I'm
written into life
by the poetry of wholeness

which sings me into being
from the deepest place.

As the water swims the fish,
and the air flies the bird,
I'm being walked by my path.

Like Walt Whitman's blade of grass
I am traced into existence
by the pilgrimage of stars.
Like this inkblot on my page
contains all the patterns of the world,
this journeywork of moonlight
transforms me and my joy
and my sorrow
into a tiny seed
of another tomorrow.

And in this state
of surrender to what wants
to become through me
I find myself
written into existence
by the earth in my bones
and the air in my lungs
and the blood in my veins
and the glow in my heart.

And so I walk the sacred walk
to good ancestorhood
of the kind which gives it forward
to the children of tomorrow

of all shapes and all sizes,
of all species and all ages
in that field beyond right and wrong.

It is the walk that
traces the fruit
and the flower in which
lies the never-ending
story of life told
by a myriad of patterns
in a multitude of places
that make up the infinite faces
of our One living world.

Now, tell me,
I am curious,
what is yours?

Two Rivers on Dartmoor

Dartmoor, Devon, June 2024

She, the plant, craves widen open beach
and fullest sun, the free dive into kelp forest
below the surface. Sterile sun is not for me today.
I want to crawl through undergrowth dappled
by mothertree canopy and sit by the darkness of Bellpool
carved into the rock foundation of the Moors.

Outer time pressure dictates that
we make it halfway and across a rickety iron bridge
on to an island off the beaten track
where there's both full sun and patchy light.

I soon have to sit down, fully dressed,
on the warm rocks by the river
cold-blooded creature that I am

shivering on a balmy midday in early June
in my long sleeve woollen top
underneath my jumper

While she is already undressed
and pushes off from the rocks,
stark naked, and out into the deeper
soft and silky sepia-tinted waters of her river,
the cold sprouting rosy flowers on her skin
revealing the life she finds
in this connection with the outer stream.

She has a gift right now I do not possess
of taking the lively onslaught on our senses
and sorting a path through the outer world
like an imaginary jetty into her river.

It is true, I am also in a river
which is why I had to sit down.
I am floating on an inner stream
beyond this space and time,
without going anywhere, it would appear.

Mine is woven of the torrent
of sense impressions
that enter me unfiltered.

The gushing and rushing and roaring
of the water over the rocks
through this steep valley
that the water's relentless flow
has eaten into the granite,

and the eddies and swirls with bubbles on,
and the fast shallow rapids of white water,
the deep pools of the mirror glass water
of slow time floating on the unbroken surface,
the green of oak trees in leaf up the steep slope,
the mosses' new and soft light green velvet
against the dark almost black of the
once-drowned carpet of last year's growth,
the ferns sprouting almost horizontally
wherever a patch of soil will hold
in a cracks of the rock face.

Heavy trees fallen years ago from those steep slopes
lie unmoved in the fast waters having
made way for new growth which finds vigorous life
in the richness of the earth curated by decades
of these veteran trees that now seem more solid
than rock in the cold water rushing by.

There is the song of a multitude of birds
and the fluttering of insects weaving their lives
into the layered patchwork quilt of this other stream
and life-giving river that I find myself immersed in,
fully dressed, at the outer water's edge,

Where I sit seemingly disconnected
by my lost and absent gaze which belies
the life going on within my alchemical laboratory and
the darkroom of my soul where the photographic plate
always lies in wait ready to capture the myriad

of outer impressions to marry them
to an inner silvery light of a different source and kind

So that from these topmost patterns and traces
etched into this upper most layer
of the world's outermost skin,
ancient histories and age-old stories
whisper to me from within:
"Give not of your time or work
but of your life so this stream of life can live."

I keep reading how some people feel
that this place of peace and solitude of mine
to them feels a cold and lonesome place.
Yet I, I feel more alone among people
who have never ventured here and do everything
they can to avoid the inner light and authority.

She has climbed out of her river
after a few minutes and dried herself.
Her skin is still cool but hair is almost dry again
and her sense of life refreshed;
it is obvious in the sparkle of her eye,
and we have been walking back a while.
We have an appointment to keep.

I don't know how much time has gone by
but something wants for me to have lingered
longer in that other stream and river,
and the stories and life still untold
are calling me to attention.

There is a deeper, timeless urgency at work
which is not so much about a length of time
but about the recognition of eternity
and that our fates are bound up with it.

The Explainer Bird

Ashburton, Devon, March 2024

This is the Explainer Bird –
a veritable bird of paradise
in his eloquence and word flushes.

He explains all day long
that he will fly and how he will fly.
Only he never flies.

It is as though his telling
is an asking for permission
which nobody gives

and nobody but he himself can give.
His whole life has become a plea
and the days have flown by

but he has been standing still,
explaining his great ambition to fly
to those who still will listen.

Once, he said to another bird,
'If you just stand here and imagine
This is a runway, I will run and take off

and I will fly this way and that.'
And, his eyes became all dreamy
as he felt in himself the longing

of great flight almost come true
and he had just begun
to open his wings when…

'I don't want you take off,' said the other bird.
'Don't fly away. I need you here.
I'm so frightened you might not return.'

His capacity to feel such pain
and hurt of others more than moved
the Explainer Bird. It arrested him.

And, he knew all the while deep inside
that there are things you cannot do
but only be, yet he never actually flew.

And, as he explained and explained
his urge to fly without actually flying,
he began to appear maybe a little stooped

and his brightly coloured plumage became
a little drab and grey, his movements a little stiff,
his appearance somehow worn beyond his days.

He concealed even to himself that
what he really dreamed of was to be let go of
rather than just actually going for it himself.

And, he was always held back
by all the reasons not to
and so he never actually did.

He never just went and flew
maybe even only in the night
or even during the day

when nobody was watching.
Not that there really was anything to keep secret
but he didn't even keep it a secret.

And, so he became a most renowned professor of flight
still having never actually flown
but having thought about flight

in every which way thought will allow
and his great thesis covered all the ways
in which a bird might fly and all the birds

ever known to have flown.
He even made a documentary
on the flight religion of birds.

All the while, he still waited for permission
for something from someone.
He himself wasn't even quite sure what or why.

The thing is that the explainer bird
was a cuckoo of a swan of a bird
in a duck's world though no swan was ever

and no cuckoo was at any time quite like he never was.
Unlike any other bird, the explainer bird
had spent his life trying to explain his way

out of a cage which he had been
carrying inside his heart since at least the time
when his mother of a duck tried to remould him

in her image, or whatever it was she was thinking or not,
when she tried to sculpt his living feathers of flight
by boiling them in molten wax

in some rage of hers sparked by
the wilful ways of a cuckoo of a swan
of a bird in a duck's world.

Then, one day, a little bird asked the explainer bird,
'Why do you always talk and never fly?
Beautiful as you talk.'

And this truth struck his heart
and plucked him from the skies
he had never known.

And, he knew there and then
that his time was over and that he had become
what he had always been and

not the weight of a single down feather more:
a lump of feathers inspired by the Great Gull of Flight
with so much potential.

QUANTICLES OF EMERGENCE

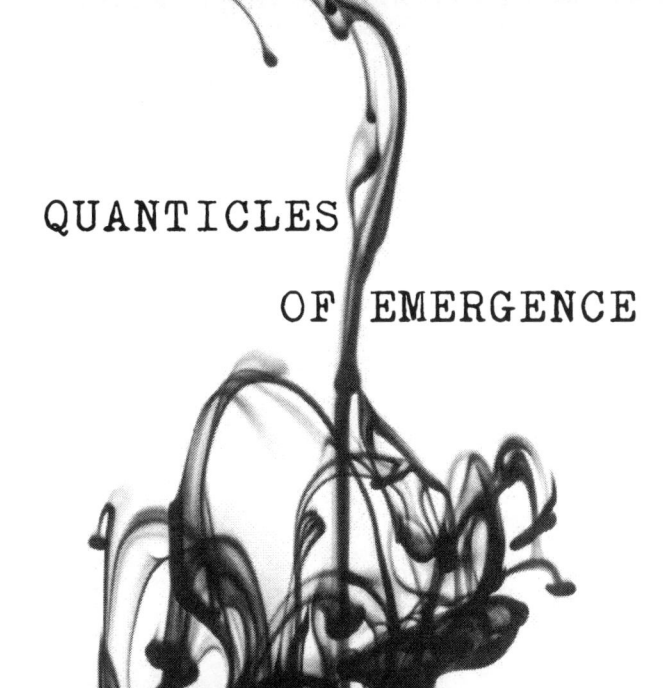

My blot of ink, this
Journeywork of moonlight

Quantum Poetry
Vol. II

Moulting

An inner pilgrimage.
Ashburton, Devon, July 2021.

I - Departure

The young man had got up more than once
and I too had rehearsed my farewells.
Yet, together we lingered over our labour,
for such a parting as ours is inevitably a death,
where the sharpness of what is lost
is so much more keenly felt, at first,
than the softness of what is new,
and what is lost will never return quite so,

Even if it is only the familiarity of old habits
for which, we are both agreed,
it is time to die. And yet, we knew them,
we knew them like our own skin,

and they were our skin, the skin we knew
from the inside, which kept us together
and in one piece and seemed to give us
our shape, and we knew nothing else.

And though we wanted to shed what it had become,
stiff and tight, restricting movement,
suffocating breath, we yet had to mourn the loss
of its protection, feel the gratitude,
have compassion with our suffering of small things
such as whether there will be enough
food on such an abundant planet as Earth,
whether we are loved in a world so full of God as ours.

II - Passage

And we reminisced, remembering the moments
when he had seen a flicker of eternity
in every passing face and how he had seen
in everything what he thought so to lack
and yearned to charm such foreign features
into his own perfection.
So, it would speak to him and through sound
and presence, closeness, suggest a unity

Of opposites, a wholesome oneness, a glimmer
to which he had attached such urgency
of creative union, believing it could last.
Though seldom such unity occurred

apart from in a giddy fog from which he would awake
not seeing that they had their own,
and he had his. His eternity. His union. His wholeness.
And that which is eternal kept on being so,

Quite undisturbed and by itself,
beyond his touch,
out of sight,
unheard,
yet nonetheless perceived.
He was always invited
by way of inkling,
always welcome.

And the two of us, we sat there just a little longer
under canopy of night and encountered things
For which the finest subtlety of word can be no match.
We stood face to face with the Ancient of
Days, and heard the Mothers' tale of death and birth,
and death and birth, and rebirth after rebirth,

And we saw the most precious things
which happened only quietly and once
and yet touched upon all things
that ever had been and ever would,
and we heard within all things
the stillness of inside forever sing
and put our fingers to that soft place
where the roof of the world
touches the bottom of all souls

and where all that seems so separate
is still unfathomable, yet already known.

Such experience seeded a thirst for life
never yet felt and any care for his temper made way
for it would no longer do, for his temper was
as ill-fitting as he had become to our shared self.

He no longer wished to be approved of, liked,
or found agreeable by some other, however close.
And such insight was his end. And my beginning.
For what I wanted then was to be understood

And permeated in every fibre by myself.
Infused by my own soul. Set alight by my spirit.
I no longer cared for justice or for peace on earth
for I realised at once that they were already here
like soul and spirit.
What mattered was what has always mattered.
Acknowledged or not.
The only thing that has ever mattered.
Whether we are capable of recognising it or not.

And now was the time to acknowledge,
to feel, to see, to drink, to witness.

III - Arrival

And, so, it came as we watched a shooting star

divide us, that final embrace.
And the worn and tired steel of his breastplate
which had concealed that he even had a heart
(Although I always knew he had one and also knew
that he wore it both to protect and to be seen)
touched against my flabby, soft chest.
I hadn't quite realised until then that despite my age

And weight and softer shape and being the one
on the face of it closer to death, I yet breathed
easier. And even in the embrace we lingered
for it was hard to part company
having known each other as well as
two can know each other
who are the present and the past of the same man.

But I did let him go, slowly, and released him
into what was his, released him
from his impatience, his vanity, his pain,
the care for his manner,
and he too let me go and passed on to me
the treasures of my younger self,
the wisdom of my youth
And between us we straightened and
folded the skin we both had known,

The skin into which he had grown and from which
I now emerged. We folded it like washer women
fold bedsheets which have dried out on the lawn
in the sun ready to be put away, properly,

in my inner airing cupboard where I put him to bed.
First, he would settle down to sleep
as if in a guest room of the main house
and I would think of him there as a safeguard

For the day when I might just again need something
protective, narrower, and more precise
to hold me upright. And, then he and I
would move on, not quite to forgetting
but to a comfort full of gratitude,
a memory, a visit with me out here,
the mystery before me, my newfound clarity within;
he safely in there, the little man, my manikin,
sliding back into the great warm darkness
with breastplate, youth, and moulted skin.

The Little Man Dancing in My Heart

Landscove, Devon, January to March 2018.

With every cockcrow
God, my Friend,
He is always singing:
"Show me around.
Show me around again."

For more than fourteen thousand daysprings
My Friend, the Little Man, has patiently
Waited by the door
Until I understood that my yearning
Was not for Him
But for me
To burst wide open
Like a rose falling apart.

That is what allowed Him
To look out of the window
Of my heart.

This morning, waking up
No longer was a chore
I did not have to drag myself
As I did before
Together from the corners of the universe.

Now I am right here and wide awake
To my Work of carrying
God, my Friend, the Little Man.
I am His royal litter, His sedan chair,
My heart His lookout
Where He leaps and crows excitedly,
"Here I already am.
Now, take me over there
Where I am becoming some more.
And over there,"
He beams pointing far ahead,
"I will have one day been so much."

The dancing makes me dizzy
And I stumble and I fall,
"Oh," God says with pity
And looks up at me,
"Please get up again.
It's through you I am.
Get up and show me around.

Show me round some more
And more and more."

And I get up and we dance
Like old lovers
Not sure whether I'm leading Him
Or He leads me.
But always in love with each other.
God in love with me and
I in love with God, my Little Friend,
Who grows and grows inside my heart,
And my heart because of Him.

We dance in and out of noon.
We dance the night away.
Towards where I will cease
And He will be
Towards my last,
His youngest day.

Bits and Pieces of the Soul

Landscove, Devon, January 2018.

There, on the floor,
sits a boy in silence staring
at a heap of shards
and splinters.

He stares as if his life depends on it.
And it does. For he thinks that the pile
is the centre of his life.
I want to reach out and tell him

what he cannot see: that
he sees it already as it is and beyond
there is nothing to see but his looking,
and by looking he holds it all in place.

And that his soul doesn't want to sit still.
And that it can't. But he will.

If only he could stare long enough, he thinks,
or at some peculiar angle, in the right way:

What seems broken
would reveal itself as whole.
The shards and splinters,
the cluttered mound of brokenness,

the many million fragments,
the bits and pieces
would arrange themselves again
into one piece, untouched,

No cracks, without a scratch,
one unity. And I have to watch him
as he stares for as long as it takes
to show that all is not as it may seem.

He wills it. He will unveil what lies
before him as some secret
as the magic shape of something special,
as wholeness in disguise.

And he scrunches up his eyes, he squints,
until he finds the angle, the point of view
with which he squeezes through the pinhole
into someone else's jumbled world.

That magic thing, that special shape,
that wondrous geometry,
he thinks he's found it, he thinks it does exist.
For as long as he is able

to maintain this twisted bond
and blame himself for thinking
he is broken when in someone else's
fact of fiction he tragic'ly is not.

For, according to his mother, the shards,
his splinters, the fragments of his broken soul,
are all perfectly assembled,
exactly when they cover up her hurt, her inner hole.

Promise of a Man

Landscove, Devon, March 2018.

Not quite the hero
I'd expected
Just a story-telling reptile

Still, a miracle perhaps, but
So much lizard
In the moment
Underneath the tailcoat

You'd be forgiven
For not seeing in between
Stretched out over a whole lifetime
So short and ill-equipped
The awkward attempt at being human

A fine morning mist

Rising from the waves
Beneath a cloudless sky

Not more than a subtle haze
Hardly material
Pierced by a ray of light

Not quite yet breath
But still
The promise of a man

Descending into Myself

Meditation for the Fool.
Begun in Heidelberg, Germany, August 2002.
Completed in Diptford, Devon, UK
between November & April 2020.

I

I read somewhere
that solitude is being alone
done well.

I'm trying. But
I'm not doing it very well.
My tiny, watery soul against

The vast night sky
that snuffs me out,

unnoticed.

And I don't know
how I keep it going. But I do.
There's the Hilliard Ensemble's Morrimur.

There's Beethoven's 5th piano concerto.
There's Rilke and the others
in my Hall of Fools.

There's two young men,
no longer quite children,
sleeping soundly and safe.

And, then, there's the page in front of me
that transforms again from artefact
into mirror.

To write, that urge
To become clear,
to understand.

I write not knowing WHAT it is
that I must write
I write knowing only THAT I must.

To shine the light on something
that I have not seen before.
(Although I may think at first that I have).

To lift it off of my soul
that I can see myself again, clearly,
getting it off my chest

and off my shoulders and on to the page.
It is often such a long way round
to that one conversation with the one

who knows me
so well: myself.

II

This flight of fancy that is me,
part conscious voyage,
mostly accidental destiny.

The topmost of the history
of so many layers
families, generations, energies

Standing on their shoulders
charged to explore some inner landscape
like the bird must navigate the outer continents.

I can inhabit perhaps only a soul's worth
of space in this landscape
from which to look out

and look back at the universe
whence I came,
but look with seeing eyes, no less.

Not driven by need to explain;
just inarticulably looking,
through eyes, inner and outer eyes.

Eyes which are like the birds' wings
and don't know which direction south is.
Eyes that blink and wings that flap

not just towards the next meal worm and woodlouse,
and back to feed the hungry chicks.
We do not know how looking goes

Or migration. We just fly and take in.
But it is more than that.
To flap and fly, to look and see: It is to be.

It is what it is to be that part-flapping,
part-flying bird, to be this part-blind,
part-seeing man, to feel connected

to this sense of meaning
which just will not reveal itself.
Who, damn it, who has given

me all these sensitivities

and then abandoned me
here, one human being,

extending 6 foot 4 and a half
into a cold universe.

III

I want to be done with the looking.
I close my eyes, and I keep still and
go within to listen to what wants out

In some awkward and haphazard way.
I am listening. I am listening to the deep silence,
the ticking of the grandfather clock,

the groaning of the roof on the old walls.
Something is hidden. I have heard the muffled voice.
In some moments everything that appears wound-up

uncoils and whispers, so close.
I sweat and suffer again.
Such great ambiguity to just sit still and wait.

That is hard work for this otherwise so vainly active mind
Which with grim and rigorous impatience faces this hard school.
Everything's in flow between the imaginary straight lines.

The answers are on the tip of my tongue
On some days. So far away on others.
As if they travelled through me or past me

quite as if they were sent out
as a distant greeting from future wisdom
from some faraway journey

sent to teach me.
I am filled briefly with a fleeting inkling
which leaves me swiftly before I can grasp it.

Then, time stands still and it appears
against the horizon of the dullness of the daily grind.
It greets me as a foreboding vaguely outlined from beyond

the wafting billows of the fog
made up of the ever-same things of my daily life.
It escapes the reach of my hands.

It blends back into the mist, disappears again.
What remains is just faint wonderment, not quite awe,
as time resumes its passing toll.

I have as yet not been able to see it clearly
and quite keep hold of it,
to stop it in its tracks.

Was it I who abandoned it
in some quiet place, somewhere,
now inaccessible to me?

Not just in the comet's tail, the shooting star, the rainbow,
or reflected in children's eyes.
Also here in the coffee cup and the long view of the
faraway horizon

Seascape or mountain view or even against a soft pillow
under a duvet against the drawn out night
or on a walk with crunching leaves under my feet,

folded in and always there, reflected, sounding:
the faintest traces, the beginning of another journey,
the first step on a path.

And I am always starting out. And never leaving.
Yet, maybe it was only a dirt track
by a quiet stream in wide open spaces,

where I left it behind
as I followed other roads.
Where could such a narrow path possibly lead?

Perhaps it becomes narrower yet
and vanishes directly into myself.
I wonder, with a sense of panic,

with this inkling that this path

indeed has no other destination.
Yet, now, still somewhat numb and deaf

I awake in unknown wonderment
Which no longer distinguishes
between suffering and joy.

All has inverted: no longer
am I compelled outside and into the world
to find the middle of all things.

I have become all over only ear
And into me flows the whole world, comes home.

IV

I am no longer submerged,
only half-conscious, half-asleep,
dreamlike yet wide awake.

At the edge of inner and outer
immersed in those things
through open eyes

and those things immersed in me;
those things which live twice,
once outside where they cease and fade;

once seen and drunken with those eyes,
taken inside and sewn seamlessly
to the infinite end of my inner milky way,

my kaleidoscopic patchwork quilt landscape
where they live on as things once seen outside
against the darkness of things yet unseen

now sounding as births of inner universes
against the silence of joyful things yet unheard
caught in the bottom

of the cup of my ear
with just one lonely tear
from those wondering eyes.

There's the light shining back at me,
obscured by dark watery depths.
It is the Original Beloved, myself,

Looking back as I look inside.
I now realise that it is I who
moved into the well within.

At home in every cell and fibre.
And I drink from this well.
I drink. I drink. I drink.

I Am Your Vessel, Not Your Captain

To my sons.
Dartington, Totnes & Broadhempston, Devon,
between May 2004 to February 2006

The universe sent out its stream of grace
to travel through my riverbed of time
towards another tomorrow
where I will have been your boat
and of which I will not be a part.

You sailed out from your mother's womb
on this river which flows towards the stars
on your journey further afield
than I will have ever been.

May I be your boat for a little while
and may you sail out, sail out far

and sail this boat that I am
and take me to my limits
may the winds howl
and the Wild Things growl
may you ride in my shelter until I break.

To where the river bends no more
where it has become the estuary
of your adolescence
where I shall sink with joy
for I have found the voice
that called me through the mists
it came from within me and now is you
may you find it too.

But before you jump and swim ashore
those foreign lands which are your home
I wish for nothing else but that
you learn to love yourself and do what you will
that is the only moral you shall hear from me
when I cite was is inscribed inside your heart.

It is you that must remind me time and time again
that I am your vessel, not your captain
for I have been sailing under your command
since long before my own adventures
to a world that once was mine and now is yours—
may you make it someone else's.

Out of the World, Into its Middle

To my sons.
Dartington, Totnes & Broadhempston, Devon,
between May 2004 to February 2006

the world does not stop its turning
for the miserable and bitter
and holds not on to those
whose heads grow heavy minded.

they must wrangle with nature's forces
who cannot but hang on anxiously
so as not to be catapulted out
into the lonely universe by the centrifuge of life.

is it not clear that
only he who is light at heart
has no need to lament his relations with gravity

for they will not keep him from
returning into the peaceful cradle
of mother nature's womb, to dissolve
into the weightless middle of the world?

THE MOON SEEKS LIFE IN THE CITY AND FINDS ONLY A POET

Poems from the Global Village

Quantum Poetry

Vol. I

The Death of the Human Situation

Dartington & Totnes, Devon,
between April & August 2004

in a concrete maze of loneliness
lit by the neon light of midnight labour
(where one hundred thousand live next door,
but are alone for no-one is a neighbour,)
in a shattered window on the 50th floor
amongst the shadows of the office towers
above the endless rows of alienation
crouched alone the human situation
gazing out into the nightly hours
past the ever sleepless banking quarters
to the lost cities' horizontal dream of happiness
that day in day out is seen in rags

seeking charity for food and drink and fags.

it contemplated long about its pain
of which most of all it hurt to be
regarded as romantic ivory
and completing what the cities had begun
- as there was nothing left but to abide -
half numb, half willed, but knowing what it did,
reached out to that severed memory
leaning forward, to jump and fly and
spread itself amongst the city-people
and sail towards its inevitably silent suicide.

All the Riches I Inherited

Dartington & Totnes, Devon,
between April & August 2004

I am a child of the lost race of the city-people
that has forgotten how to live
and, in vain, has aspired to those feelings
that you cannot have but only be,
amongst which are happiness, and life, and liberty.
my thoughts often now go back in time
to where, although young and unqualified,
already as a child I had a memory
of an unencountered disposition
to be free and happy and alive
that we cannot learn, but only be.
and since then I have spent my days
wandering with this yearning for a place

where I as an individual could live
and in a landscape have a home amongst a people
a place to return to from my travels
hands to shake, arms to hold, bodies to embrace
where I was a human amongst other human beings
a companion, a neighbour and a friend
but however much I travelled
I had to find that roads that leave a city only find another
and I am tired now of searching for chance and possibility
but to never seize the opportunity to live
and by accumulating possibilities
have reduced my happiness to an unreliable future issue
too
if it is not already buried with love, and trust, and individuality
in my disconnected childhood memory

By the Grace of My True Yearning, For What I Am It Has No Price

Dartington & Totnes, Devon,
between April & August 2004

I am a river and a river
flows through me.
It's not that I am lazy.
I just despise all effort
beyond being
what I already am,
my true nature.

There are forces at work in me
great and without name

and although I cannot conceive of them
I follow them. I am them, day-by-day.

Have you seen the water mill turned?
Have you seen the rocks
that crumbled under my persistence?
Have you seen the creatures
whose thirst I quenched?

Without effort I have melted
in the mountains
and flowed joyfully
as a stream
giving rise
to lush meadows
in spring.

And without effort,
I have melted
not just the ice
atop the mountain.
I have melted
the mountain itself
and I have shaped it
as it has shaped me.

I have fertilised
my delta with the sea
I am what happens to me
and I am what happens through me.

What forms another,
forms each other,
forms itself, forms me.

For there are forces at work in me
great and without name
and although I cannot conceive of them
I follow them. I am them, day-by-day.

I am a river and a river
flows through me.
It's not that I am lazy.
I just despise all effort
beyond being
what I already am,
my true nature.

I journey on towards my gravity.
I flow on not asking for permission,
drawn in and drawing in,
according to the nature of the territ'ry,
up and down, crashing into rocks
and filling basins, waiting patiently
'til, drop-by drop, I grow out of this
or that depression,
my meniscus crawling upward
steadily towards some higher edge,
still out of sight until flowing over,
flowing on,
splashing over rims,

into crevices,
I overcome all obstructions.

I overcome inner and outer imprisonment
and with renewed fervour
I will forever flow
into every freedom
through any rock
and over any field,
for I do not bend
at anyone's command
– not even my own –
if often I wished I would.

I am a river and a river
flows through me.
It's not that I am lazy.
I just despise all effort
beyond being
what I already am,
my true nature.

And I have run dry
more than once.
I have evaporated
to travel with the skies.
Have you ever seen me
travel in the clouds?
And then my tears conspired
to further my path sometimes

with a rumbling torrent, sometimes
with the gentlest of silent drizzles
always independent of my lower wanting
and certainly of any lesser morality.

I have tried to listen and to learn
but there are ways in which
I cannot be educated
and the following of straight lines
has been the greatest waste of time

for I have no ulterior goal and destination
beyond flowing and flooding,
beyond my gushing and rushing,
beyond my drop and trickle.

I puddle and sit and
eddy and rush and stream on,
effortlessly, to sea and ocean
whence I come and where I lose my name
and all distinctions and yet return
to my source which becomes my mouth
in wave and tide and seaglass mirror
to moonshine, sunrise and shooting star alike.

Even through you, dear City,
who treats all of my kin with contempt
and wants to imprison and harvest
what it does not understand,
I flow through you

for the short while
that you last
and carry forth your filth and waste
and wash away
your stench of death.

You send me your moneyman
to measure my value
in utility and time.
It is the biggest crime.
But I bear your evaluation
by the grace of my true yearning,
which knows not of certificate and paper
and which to you is worthless
for what I am, it has no price.
I am one of the five you are made of,
air, fire, earth, water and space.

Yet, after you've measured me up
you straighten my edges
you redirect me
you pollute me
you curse me
for the floods and droughts
that you have caused yourself
in the name of what you call prosperity
which is but the death of life
and the death of me.

Yet, I still live on for I am free

beyond the bounds
of your limitations in time
and I am determined by forces
beyond your grasp
even when you turn my waters
lifeless and murky and muddy,
I still dissolve, and I drag along,
I nibble, and I quench,
I ooze, and I float,
I lap, and I fill,
and I crash, and I wet.

I carry every piece of driftwood,
if it has patience enough, to its beach,
and I do not care whether it is steep
or flat, whether you swim in me,
or drown, whether you mock
my shallow waters
or build a dam to make use of me.

There are forces at work in me
great and without name
and although I cannot conceive of them
I follow them. I am them, day-by-day.
I am not lazy, I despise all effort
beyond my nature.

My drops seeps through any stone.
I follow a different kind of time.
Through soil and into root and out of leaf

towards cloud and down down down again.

I am a river and a river
flows through me.
It's not that I am lazy.
I just despise all effort
beyond being
what I already am,
my true nature.

My Gallows Star

Dartington & Totnes, Devon,
between April & August 2004

I am welded to some distant realm
– unknown and unknowable, perhaps –
through a rope of light let down to me
by some wretched star immersed in utter darkness
and this darkness that makes it shine
also is the cause for our separation
for my star with all its light is heaven bound
from where it lures me with its ideals
polluting all my thinking with its fancy theory
of, oh, how different life could be
while I, here, at the other end of darkness,
retained by the practised way things are
still routinely walk on earthly ground

that is the cause of all my misery

that this rope of light soon formed a knot
of hope and fear around my neck
and the resulting noose of time
has since been fastening

and in that it is but consolation that
my gravity now lies with my dreams
for while my star draws me ever closer
this earth's forces too cling on to me
and in this, my pending human situation,
determined by despair and captivation
with my identity stretched out between the two
I put this, my own humble life, forward
as an offering to some greater cause

while I remain hanging from my gallows star
I sometimes question the meaning of it all
and timidly pinch my arm, from time to time,
thinking to myself, "It cannot be."
but also know for sure that, "No, I am not dead."
at least not here, not now, not yet.
and as I gently swing, dangling
from the rope of light around my neck
I feel I have been lifted off the ground
an inch not more and yet I am already
on my journey t'wards the universe
by the graceful light of my gallows star

between the heavens and the earth
things are gradually compromised:

they are not how they could be
but already better than they were
for what once seemed dilemma now is me
and from an unknown place within
the calming knowledge gently rises
that, indeed, "I am alive! I am alive!"
just, for now, suspended in eternal crisis.
and although my self remains forlorn
as a seeker I now have become my own creator
and a universal rumour has it that one day
this self, it will be born. "I will be born."

THIS EXQUISITELY
TERRIFYING JOLT

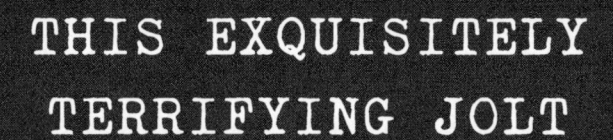

On the Origin and
Meaning of
Quantum Poetry

Quantum Poetry
Epilogue

This Exquisitely Terrifying Jolt

An Essay by Way of an Epilogue
On the Origin and Meaning of Quantum Poetry
Ashburton, Devon, July 2024

This essay began with the intent to pen a foreword to point the reader of my poetry towards related aspects and insights which it feels a great shame not to share. For example, what I say about the meaning of the title of the collection along with other various references to the moon throughout the book and some biographical references bring to life not just an additional layer. They bring the whole collection together into a more complete form of the universe which I have come to inhabit consciously. My writing is an illustration of this place from within. My work is very much about the inwardness of things. It is about what things mean to me, what they feel like to me, about my experience of being alive.

It has been said that, in contrast to my poetry, my essays come across as more intellectual and less heartfelt. There is then the worry, quite legitimately, that an essay might get in the way of the poems.

However, against this worry, I have the hope that, at least for some, this additional essay-layer can provide more of the lodestone quality that I myself look for in a book. The kind of thing that goes in and transforms me, that gives voice to and inspires the life in me and my creative agency. I mean the kind of book that is so transporting that I come out of it, so to speak, as a different individual than I go into it. That, to me, is one of the greatest gifts of life and that is what I am exploring here.

Nonetheless, as the completion of this book approached, I decided entirely in favour of the poetry, and this essay became the epilogue.

On behalf of that which goes by many names and which inspired me to write in the first place, I am humbled by and grateful to you for opening yourself to this book and for allowing the words to take you on a journey. As I say it in "The Sacred Oath of the Quantum Poet" on page 45:

And I thank you
for this audience
that I might sing to you
of this question
which is also my oath
in which I pledge,
first of all, that
I may hear it,
and then that I may know
what it means.

Eventually, through a strange series of jolts and portal experiences my soul and I, we found our cosmic home address at the intersection of a plethora of works by various cultural creatives – artists, composers, poets, writers, architects, thinkers, and such like. They are works and people who I'll refer to, collectively, as the *Depth and Transcendence Tradition* within Western culture.

Depth and Transcendence Tradition is a label I have made up, as far as I am aware, in order to lump together a defiant, rebellious and life-giving melange of voices which form a counter choir to the dominant devitalising institutional cacophony of contemporary Western culture.

This Western culture is many beautiful things and it is, sadly, also home to a few, at best, superficial and, at worst, toxic perspectives which make up the chapters of *The Story of No Story* as I call it in my book *Keystones in the Patterns of Place*: rationalism, materialism, secularism, linearism, mechanism, utilitarianism, pragmatism, individualism. It's a long list of fragmented and deadened abstractions which are yet held together powerfully by a low-level of collective consciousness and the violence it does to each and every one of us who have had their heart and soul not just repressed but amputated by some of what has happened in the years of what is called socialization, culturalization, and education, at home and at school.

I have come to the view that the main problem is that the history of the West is a history of an ever-increasing institutionalisation in all aspects of human affairs, which is inevitably accompanied by a corresponding loss of individual human agency. If you want to survive in a collective without your own agency, you need to cut yourself off from your feelings, for that will hurt less for a while than to have the feelings in the first place.

This is why my phrase *Depth and Transcendence Tradition* is an oxymoron which needs to be treated with care. Whilst it is clearly a wisdom tradition of its own kind, it is as far from a collective as you could possibly get, and that also means that it must not be confused with individualism which is just another collective. It is about the uniqueness of individual human agency as it happens to arise and flower in each of us.

Human agency, in my experiences, is a consequence of the clarity not of where I am going but of where I am coming from. The individual works that I am lumping together into the *Depth and Transcendence Tradition* have in common that they are lodestones. They are transporting and transformative. They tell me not what to do but they help me appreciate who I am.

The purpose of such true human agency in my case, as far as I have been able to understand it, is about the exploration of my feeling life, not in the sense of living at the whim of my base emotions, but about the possibility of being of service to life. As long as I am disconnected from my feeling life, I am unable to truly be of service to life.

Another way of putting it is that there is a place where beauty and life are the same thing, and I have come to believe that, at least for me, any sense of personal ethics or true individual human agency can only come from this place.

Human agency, however, is of course a phrase that is hard to comprehend from an institutional perspective, not least because individual human agency is what institutions need to both keep at bay and redeploy in order to make the life energy contained within individual humans (and any other life form!) available for their own purposes.

Beyond merely acknowledging the possibility of a sense of depth, meaning, and sacredness of the human experience, the *Depth and Transcendence Tradition* is about being in service to life through nurturing the heart and soul. It is about a profound, exploration of the relational, embodied, spiritual, archetypal, and transcendent aspects of being human. These aspects together make up what has been called the *vertical dimension* of human existence, or its *vertical axis*. At the top of this vertical dimension of our lives, we will flower and fade yet, even in our death, the petals of our lives will fall to the ground and meet our roots to feed yet more life. So, we live on and give it forward at the same time.

I believe that it is the loss of this sense of the vertical dimension in the course of our Western cultural biography that we suffer like the loss of a limb or an organ, the nature of which we cannot recall, yet we suffer its absence in the most existential way. It is a sickness we all carry in us and yet we hardly know how to feel it, describe it, or even make sense of it. We are not capable of these things because the organ which gives us these capabilities to feel and to experience and to articulate it has been removed.

In my attempts at getting in touch with this organ and the vertical axis of my living human existence, I have been on a fool's journey for the longest time, winding my way through subjects as far apart as mysticism and economics, depth psychology and music theory, ecology and metaphysics, computing and sociology, poetry and agriculture, mathematics and philosophy, to name but a few.

It has been a long pilgrimage to a place of just enough clarity to realise that my journey, in turn, is not a mirror of the fragmentation of Western culture brought about by my hopelessly hyperactive mind. Rather, there is, in fact, an integrative and holistic method to this madness. The active agent in this journey is not my mind; it is my soul that wants to be born despite the best efforts to sabotage its incarnation from within and without.

There is an interconnected and yet transcendent wholeness that is addressed by each separate subject that catches my interest and each subject finds ways of connecting to the others through my appreciation. At the intersection, they weave what is sometimes referred to as the mythopoetic matrix, a technical term for the soul, and that is my cosmic home address.

My poem *My Gallows Star* included as the last poem in *Vol. I* (page 108) goes some way to articulate this soul birthing experience. It ends with the defiant certainty that

*a universal rumour has it that one day
this self, it will be born. "I will be born."*

The essence of *My Gallows Star* is reflected in *My Wyrd Awakening* which opens *Vol. III* (page 16). For example, its fourth part, on page 40, opens with a description of the birth of myself which now, twenty years after writing *My Gallows Star*, brings a whole other dimension of experience and subtlety of exploration to yet the same thing:

*I fell
through the membrane
at the edge of psyche
and matter
and cleft open
the wound there
of my selfhood
which bleeds
with the time
I am made of
and which I exude,
like a starry pinprick
in the vast sky
must bleed
with the light
of its star.*

The multi-layered, multi-faceted and transdisciplinary meandering and weaving of the soul-birthing process in me, or at least something like that, was observed by a fellow pilgrim on my way to the cathedral of St. Francis of Assisi in September 2021 when he dubbed me the *Quantum Poet*[i].

We were walking the St. Francis trail from Piediluco to Assisi together with a group of fellow pilgrims under the leadership of the modern mystic Sujith Ravindran.

Sujith has given much time to exploring the parallels and direct correspondences between the language and notions of quantum mechanics, consciousness and the ancient wisdom traditions of the world, especially of his native India. The understanding this enables is of quantum science as a modern wisdom tradition.

Quanta as specific energy packets, the uncertainty principle, the notion of superstates, the wave-particle duality, quantum jumps, and entanglement – these are all also ways of understanding consciousness and ways of seeing and being in the world. They point to the Jung-Pauli conjecture of the final non-duality and unity of psyche and matter which does not reduce psyche and consciousness to an epiphenomenon of a material world but uplifts matter to an ever-flowing expression of a superstate of possibility and potential of being.

In quantum mechanics there is the possibility of journeying not only within the coherence of spacetime but also in jumps, so called quantum jumps, from one location to another without the passing of time or the passing through space, and such leaps involve the spontaneous generation of vast amounts of energy.

This reality of motion is in defiance of the classical mechanistic conception of the universe which assumes an order of particles in space and time. It essentially sees us and everything as cogs inside of an enormous clockwork, the order of which is determined by linear strings of cause and effect. *Cause-effect* is, in fact, the central metaphor of the *universe-as-clockwork myth* of classical physics with its emphasis on linearity and mechanism.[vii]

We can now trace back the two conceptions of the workings of the universe, *classical physics* on the one hand and *quantum mechanics* on the other, to their parallel in the structure of the two hemispheres of our brain and the two resulting broad narrative perspectives of the world which they give rise to[viii].

These two storylines are not just narratives but more aptly described as modes of being. In my forthcoming book *Keystones in the Patterns of Place*, I refer to these two ways of being in the world as *The Story of Another Tomorrow* and *The Story of No Story*.

There is an important and direct relationship between this collection of my poetry here and my book of interconnected essays *Keystones in the Patterns of Place*. Both use the English language, but they do so in a very different way. My essays look from the outside in. My poetry looks the other way. It is about inwardness. Though I speak about both in poems and essays, the very structure of the language beyond the individual words, they both, structurally, appeal to, enable and emphasise one perspective and one kind of consciousness, respectively.

As Iain McGilchrist illustrates so poignantly, in contrast to the literal nature of the left hemisphere of our brain structure, the capacity to work with language that enables metaphors and symbols relies on the right hemisphere. This is not necessarily only a question of style. It is also a question of transcending and integrating themes across different disciplines from different perspectives. The holistic perspective emerges from the right hemisphere which alone is capable of seeing things in context.

McGilchrist's essential work, *The Master and His Emissary*, gives us an insight into the fate and trajectory of Western culture and its interdependence with the structure of the human brain. In his book, he demonstrates the equally terrifying and liberating insight that the evolution of our brain structure towards an increasing left-hemisphere dominance has been playing out in Western history and already twice before, with the Ancient Greeks and Romans, led to the end of the imperial way of civilisation.

But it is precisely this structure of our brain and its asymmetrical division into the left and right hemispheres which, when grasped for its existential reality, is also able to provide us with the way out of this predicament and to turn the curse into a blessing. Buried underneath so much else, there is after all a beautiful gift in Western culture even though it, first, takes the recovery of the amputated organ and our feeling life to redeem it.

The *vertical dimension* of human existence, translated into neuroscience, reveals that we absolutely need the left hemisphere of our brains. It also tells us that we need it with the right attitude. We need the left hemisphere, but we need it as a faithful servant leader in service of life, not as a tyrant who brings the sixth extinction event and climate change and then cannot find a way out of these compound crises. This is where our left hemisphere dominance has taken us. This is why the much-quoted observation, sometimes attributed to Albert Einstein, is entirely correct: we will not find our way out of this crisis by way of the same kind of thinking that got us into it.

Where the left hemisphere depends on direct, sequential expressions and literal language to clarify meaning, the right hemisphere's insights often require metaphors and vaguer narratives for expression. Yet, in our culture, which favours explicitness and often views such explicitness as a mark of truth, the nuanced, metaphorical language of the right hemisphere is, at best, undervalued, mostly misunderstood as mere myth and fable or, at worst, decried as downright lie and falsehood – that is, of course, if we can still hear it in such a way that it makes any intelligible sense in the first place.

By way of example, I will jump straight to the paradox created by rationality and faith. Our left-hemisphere dominant interpretation of history has led us to believe that rationality is opposed to belief and faith. It appears, however, that we are here, once more, in the grip of the left-hemisphere understanding of the world. As McGilchrist explains, where "the right hemisphere's view is inclusive, 'both/and', synthetic, integrative; it realises the need for both. The left hemisphere's view is exclusive, 'either/or', analytic and fragmentary – but, crucially, unaware of what it is missing. It therefore thinks it can go it alone."[ix]

When there is a generative collaboration between the two hemispheres, according to McGilchrist, "neurological research reveals a consistent picture of how the two hemispheres contribute to the richness of experience. Essentially this is that the right hemisphere tends to ground experience; the left hemisphere then works to clarify, 'unpack' and generally render the implicit explicit; and the right hemisphere finally reintegrates what the left hemisphere has produced with its own understanding, the explicit once more receding, to produce a new, now enriched, whole."[x]

This healthy collaboration of the two ways of being in the world of our left and right hemispheres of our brain produce a *third way*, a perspective and way of being which is the integration of the two into a greater whole. Objectivity and subjectivity become intersubjectivity. The deep and detailed understanding of things transcends the "death by data" and the meaninglessness of metrics and, instead, becomes a way of appreciating interconnectedness, oneness and the flows of existence. Two simple and down to earth examples of how this might work in reality are the understanding in ecology of the trophic cascade or of how the four ecosystem processes – the solar cycle, the water cycle, the mineral cycle, and community dynamics – allow us to understand the health or lack thereof in any of the ecosystems on which life depends.

This way, our detailed experiences can take place with a context and frame, allow for the relationship between the inner sense of subject to the outer world, create self and other, experience intersubjectivity, explore things in great conscious detail, and then make possible the work of returning the infinitesimal fractal nature of discrete data gained through the left-hemisphere into the bigger picture of life, wholeness and conscious interconnectedness provided by the right.

This is the work that, above all else, allows us to experience the parallel greatness and limitation of our consciousness, another prerequisite for our capacity to place ourselves into a role of service to life.

When we earnestly go about it, it delivers us the possibility of a kind of vision of transformation at the centre of the cosmos in which we are involved as individual human agents. Where the institutional view holds that it is significance that matters and thus leads us into competition and scarcity as the dominant storylines, the experience of embodied human agency comes with the recognition that we are small but that we are also relevant to the wholenesses to which we belong, that wholeness leads to abundance, and that interconnectedness is a form of cosmic collaboration.

I have experienced in myself a phenomenon I call *God's great lightning conductor*. Like any conductor, this is a vertical rod or axis, and this one happens to run through me. It is bounded by two extremes at either end, heaven above and the earth beneath my feet so-to-speak, and, between these endpoints, life flows through me quite fluidly across five distinct experiential layers to make up a total of seven aspects within the wholeness that is my feeling life.

The full possibility and range of feeling surely is infinitely subtle and to speak of any layers, levels or gradations is a grave injustice to the true phenomenon. Yet, beyond my idiosyncratic conception of seven layers of feeling, lies something more profound. But, I have also found it pleasurable and satisfying to see a connection between my axis of feeling, the seven chakras as observed in the Indian tradition, the seven heavenly spheres as observed by the European alchemists, and the seven endocrine glands of the human body. It is my personal way of exploring the experience of the simultaneous coexistence of such a breadth of consciousness whilst also recognising its evolutionary path within my own life, within the cultural sense and in the widest possible sense from the evolution of the universe to that of life on Earth: they are all present in the here and now of my body.

Humans of all cultures and all times have described systems of wholeness and interconnectedness based on a variety of number systems – three, four, five, seven, ten, twelve, and others. And, these divisions make the vertical axis what it is. Call it a compass which enables orientation in the world across space and time which allows us to experience ourselves as having meaning and purpose including having a role as a custodial species which mediates between the realms of the sky and of the earth as, for example, the Aboriginal Australians articulated it.

Without such a compass, when the vertical axis has been removed and flattened by a reduction to a mere function of lifeless matter, we become an absurd accident without purpose floating disconnectedly in empty space.

But back to *God's great lightning conductor*: whatever the number of its subdivisions, I believe it is fair to say that it is aligned with the experience of most of us that feeling exists along the spectrum from where it is entirely outside of us and disowned and from where it might lead to an increasingly differentiated experience which enables us to relate to the world.

We move from feeling as something we can barely and at best intermittently tolerate to something that we actively invite to guide us and which helps us to understand what we avoid, to recognise patterns, to locate anomalies, to identify desirables and undesirables, to order our thoughts and priorities, and what we want to focus on, to experience such a thing as purpose and how to align our actions with it. We become increasingly capable of valuing both positive and negative feeling.

Beyond this, we likely all have experienced that feeling can assume the possibility of an immediate intimacy and that we are able to permit our feeling to become a journey that we can go on. This is something that, for me, is both hard to bear and something I often look for.

The feeling, whether positive or negative, takes me somewhere and I am able to fully live inside the fullest subjectivity of the experience. From here it is only a small step into the web of the interpersonal and intersubjective nature of the feeling field which exists not just between me and other human beings. It exists between everything that exists now, that has ever existed and that will ever exist. In fact, the simplistic conception of time as a linear arrow between the past, the present and the future breaks down for me when I am in this space. It is a space of interconnection which has been described as the *Third Area* by the psychologist Nathan Schwartz-Salant[xi] or as *interbeing* by Thich Nhat Hanh[xii].

I am both in a simultaneous state of being dissolved and united with what is around me whilst still retaining my distinct sense of subjectivity and consciousness. I am part of the All but also the One experiencing the All. It is a surrender to the reality of becoming within my own life and between the lives of those before and after me.

In the context of holism, this has once been described to me as the parallel state of *outer openness* and *inner coherence*. I have identity and agency whilst I am also interconnected. In fact, my identity and agency are intimately, inseparably and proportionately linked to this interconnectedness.

This, to me, is the phenomenon of being like a keystone – very much in the ecological sense – over and through which the waters of life flow in such a way that my inevitable footprint is not a thing to avoid but a dynamic force that in its wake generates more life. (This is the whole meaning behind the title of my book *Keystones in the Patterns of Place*.)

Against this explication of the gradation of my own experience of the feeling function I hope it makes sense when I say that the possibilities of being human, to me, then are connected directly to the possibilities of the wider world in its widest possible cosmic sense. This connection comes about through my capacity for feeling. That which relates me to this world is the fullest variety and possibility of my human connection through the breadth of my capacity for feeling. The more I feel, the more subtle I am able to reach into my feelings, the more subtle I am able to reach into the world.

My poems share with most of my writing at least two qualities: they are something in their own right with their own life, and they are, at the same time, the footsteps and traces left behind by my revisiting and exploring a seminal experience I had first around the age of eight. It followed my induction into the world of armchair travel and magic-carpet flight under the instruction and role modelling of my maternal grandfather. Dressed in but pyjamas, him in an armchair, me on his lap, and a duvet on me, he spent days upon days reading to me or staring into the distance together in the rare gift of comfortable silence. I later discovered that such staring is just another way of reading another kind of pattern. But that is a story for another day.

From then on, I have repeatedly experienced a peculiar phenomenon when I came into contact with the works of the creatives within what I have labelled the *Depth and Transcendence Tradition* including books, films, sculptures, paintings, buildings, gardens, landscapes, and music of a certain kind. One of the characteristics of the experience is its transporting nature which follows a thunderbolt moment which goes to my core. While this exquisitely terrifying jolt lasts, my consciousness seems to leave its familiar tracks. An awful lot and nothing happen at the same time. I am aware that a lot of something is happening, but the rush and nature of images, sounds, and meaning elicited by the outer stimulus – yet occurring on my inside – is beyond my conscious grasp. I can grasp only that I cannot grasp it whilst I also grasp that there is something tremendous beyond me that I am involved with. It is a moment of simultaneous deep pleasure and awe which includes the overwhelming terror of an encounter with something far greater than I am capable of understanding.

My humble journey to something akin to a little taste of greater consciousness has not been a linear and gradual affair. It has manifested in these kinds of leaps and bounds against a background of increasing awareness of my interconnectedness and entanglement with the world.

In this way and through these jolts, I have been permitted to glimpse the timeless *superposition of enlightenment* every so often as discrete quanta or packets of creational insights have constellated a modest quantum leap in my consciousness. These experiences are portal moments of something which we might technically describe as *complex kinaesthesia*. Previously disconnected realms of experience and knowledge become entwined and assume a new depth of life and knowledge. *The Tree of Life* and *the Tree of Knowledge* grow together, after all.

In *Two Rivers on Dartmoor*, page 56, I have captured this feeling in one particular way:

I sit seemingly disconnected
by my lost and absent gaze which belies
the life going on within my alchemical laboratory and
the darkroom of my soul where the photographic plate
always lies in wait ready to capture the myriad
of outer impressions to marry them
to an inner silvery light of a different source and kind

Somehow, through these narrative, poetic, visual and/or musical portals, there is the possibility of leaping into the inside of the world where things are connected. With Jan Christian Smuts, we might call it *inwardness*[xiii] which is the thing which becomes greater as *wholeness*[xiv] increases and its rigid structures become looser, giving rise to outer and inner life, from physical and mineral to ecological, biological and psychic, all the way through to the flower of consciousness.

The experience I am referring to communicates something about the nature and order of the world. There is something in the storyline, dialogue, and word order, or in the arrangement of music or colours in a painting, the shape of a sculpture or performance which articulates and communicates something essential which I recognise as true about the way the world is patterned and ordered at a deeper level beyond its surface. I recognise then that my own being is patterned in that same way. I understand then that my being is induced by a greater wholeness by an eternally ongoing flow of life. In this way, the alignment of patterns in the storyline and poetic use of language or rhythm and harmony of the music reach into me and trigger an archetypally true experience – a recognition of my shape and place in the world.

Yet still, for some, the observations of the outer world described by quantum mechanics and the subjective experiences of inner world should not be conflated. It is anti-scientific, they say. But then others see precisely in this conflation the of complexity science which makes human emotions and feelings – subjectivity par excellence – a central component of such scientific enquiry.

The architect and design theorist Christopher Alexander once said that there are two approaches to God: faith and reason. "Faith works easily when it is present," he said. "Reason is much harder. […] Yet in 20th century discourse reason is almost the only way we have of explaining a difficult thing so that another can participate."[xv]

Alexander speaks of his biography in terms that we might, at first, all recognise: childhood as the naïve wholeness of childhood, a primitive faith, followed by adolescence and apprenticeship in dark forests of non-understanding. But then, Alexander describes his journey culminating in the emergence of an understanding which is both "visionary and empirical […] which has roots in primitive faith, and from it builds bridges of logic and scientific coherence towards a new kind of visionary faith rooted in scientific understanding."[xvi]

Alexander is one of those who holds that for science to be true to what we are, what the world is, and what our role in it might be, we need to rely on more than dispassionate reason: we need to bring our feelings into our approach to life as a central anchor. In his articulation of a holistic approach to science, our feelings are so central that they make or break our connection to life. "This new kind of faith and understanding," he says, "is based on a new form of observation. It depends, for its success, on our faith (as human beings) that our feelings are legitimate."[xvii]

To put it another way, we cannot have ethics without faith and no faith without feeling. Feeling is what gives us the capacity to value and evaluate what matters. Feeling allows us to prioritise and focus our actions. Feeling allows us to order our thoughts and relationships with ourselves, with each other and the world.

Feeling, faith and reason meet at a fine edge which forms a pivot point on which our relationship with the world tips this way or that. As E.F. Schumacher has beautifully articulated it, what seems to matter here is the realisation that there are actually two kinds of science at work where Western culture, since Descartes and Bacon, has acknowledged only one. A drastic shift has occurred from what Schumacher refers to as *science for understanding* – the purpose of which 'was the enlightenment of the person and her 'liberation' – to *science for manipulation* – the purpose of which is *power*[xviii]. We now know these two sciences by different names. We call the one wisdom and the other science, respectively, and the belief is that only science is connected to truth. While it is inevitably a much more complex matter than that, this is what our reductive soundbite culture propagates.

It is a culture that readily dismisses conceptions of reality that transcend manipulative, functional, utilitarian, quantitative approaches to knowing, hence my calling its narrative *The Story of No Story*. It cuts the numinous off at the root by folding it back into the materialistic way of understanding things. Anything that ventures too far from the fold is reigned back in by being reduced to a mere epiphenomenon. In this way, Western culture is by and large stuck on a level of function, value and *doing*, unable to experience *ways of being* when, ironically, that is precisely what it yearns for, or so it seems to me if my experience is anything to go by.

Is this blot of ink on the page before me indeed just a random clumsy accident and does my writing process take part entirely separately from it? Or is there a light beyond or even within the inkblot that may become available to me if I engage with it and sit with it rather than move on from it or even eradicate it?

The alchemists' experience of the order of the heavens understood the moon as the mediating layer between Earth and the higher orders of the universe all the way to the Sun. The wisdom of lunar consciousness and its light could be harvested in small drops of dew.[xix]

This rich symbolism connects the lunar rhythms and cycles which influence embodied life on Earth so profoundly with the feminine and the element of water and through these nested layers of symbols to our embodied feeling life inside and to nature outside of us.

The whole of our psyche becomes a feeling-toned microcosm which we can come into relationship with and in turn, through it, we can come into direct relationship with the macrocosm around us. This deep exploration of human embodiment and of the feeling-life is one of the facets of the alchemical tradition that sets a sharp counterpoint to the dominant worldviews in Western history which denounced the body, the senses, and nature, along with its emotions and feelings, and femininity per se.

With regard to our inner lives, the Rorschach inkblot test[xx] is a phenomenological example of the meaning, purpose and the possibility of access to otherwise unavailable thoughts and feelings through which we can explore our fullness. They are not only part of our fullness; they are a foundational component of the *vertical dimension and axis* of human experience.

With regard to our outer lives, Benoit Mandelbrot's fractal geometry, especially the famous Mandelbrot Set also named the inkblot or inkbrot[xxi], is an example of how we can relate to the complexity and aesthetics of nature.

Walt Whitman, in his *Song of Myself,* wrote that *"I believe that a leaf of grass is no less than the journey-work of the stars"*[xxii]. His extraordinary poetry gave voice to the beautiful experience of the interconnectedness of the universe, from the smallest elements of nature to the vast cosmos. His poetic metaphor brings together the inner and outer into a knowing and experience of the unity.

Standing on Whitman's shoulders and borrowing his phraseology, my inkblot becomes the journeywork of moonlight. It has been my task for the longest time to discover the light within and beyond my *Inkblot Moon*. On the journey, I have harvested so much of my awareness of life by making sense of my own inkblots and those of others, literal and metaphorical, and I cannot refrain from listing a few to bring to life a very special experience that they have made possible for me repeatedly.

In chapter 7 of his *The Wind in the Willows*[xxiii], Kenneth Grahame describes how Mole has what I am calling a portal experience when he and Rat go looking for Otter's son, Portly, who has gone missing. Rat and Mole get in their boat and row through the night when, just before dawn, they come across an incredible music. They walk through trees and come face-to-face with a deity who is clearly the great god Pan, though he is not named.

"Then suddenly the Mole felt a great Awe fall upon him, an Awe turned his muscles to water, bowed his head, and rooted his feet to the ground. It was no panic terror - indeed he felt wonderfully at peace and happy - but it was an awe that smote and held him and, without seeing, he knew it could only mean that some august Presence was very, very near."[xxiv]

Grahame describes the experience in exquisite detail which is then concluded by "the gift of forgetfulness."[xxv] Rat and Mole awake as though from sleep only to find the otter boy right there on the ground. Mole is aware of a dream he cannot remember, while Rat notices hoof prints in the grass: They then load the boy into the boat and take him back to his family recognizing that they have had an unusual if elusive experience.

Saint-Exupéry's *The Little Prince* delivered another portal experience when, on the anniversary of his arrival on planet Earth, the Little Prince decides to return home as his home planet once again aligns with Earth. He decides to transition between the two worlds aided by the highly symbolic bite of a snake.[xxvi]

Bach's *Jonathan Livingston Seagull*, who has been made outcast by his flock for seeking to explore the world of flight beyond mere survival, finds himself travelling the outer world until he transitions into his inner world and their discovers, at first reluctantly, a flock of a different kind.

Having searched for most of his life up until this point for perfect speed and having always encountered limitations, the wise elder Chang teaches him the nature of limitless flight by being in the moment as an incarnation of the Great Gull.[xxvii]

Tolkien's *The Smith of Wootton Major* tells of the smith who as a boy, accidentally or so it seems, by eating a slice of cake and ingesting a magical star which becomes affixed to his brow yet "few people in the village noticed it though it was not invisible to attentive eyes."[xxviii]

As *Starbrow* he is able to journey to the land of *Faery* where he "was welcome [...]; for the star shone bright on his brow, and he was as safe as a mortal can be in that perilous country."[xxix]

The story goes on to describe the "things of both beauty and terror that he could not clearly remember nor report to his friends, though he knew that they dwelt deep in his heart. But some things he did not forget, and they remained in his mind as wonders and mysteries that he often recalled."[xxx]

Whenever I re-read the passage of this story in which the smith realises that it is time to give up the star which makes him *Starbrow* and return it so that another child can receive the gift[xxxi], I find myself bursting into tears (providing that I am on my own as I cannot, in general, cry in the company of others).

My childhood edition of Michael Ende's *The Neverending Story* was printed in red ink for those parts which describe one of the story's heroes, Bastian, in the so-called real world and green ink for those parts of the story which take place in *Fantastica*.

As the story progresses, Bastian approaches the precipice between the worlds where he is challenged to intervene and cross a particular kind of line for, if he does not, the story will repeat forever and never be able to continue. The story makes it clear to him that his own agency is at stake. His very own imagination and generativity of thought and feeling is what determines the future of the world, for if he does not dare, the Great Nothing which is taking over humankind will tear Fantastica apart.[xxxii]

My long-poem *Wyrd Awakening* which opens this collection begins, in the poem's first part entitled *The Boy Receives an Invitation,* with this layered portal experience of my encounter with *The Neverending Story.*

It describes the precipice at the edge of one world and another, and the transition across the boundary in some detail, and then goes on to connect it with other portal experiences.

The poem refers to Marie Louise von Franz's beautiful analysis of the patterns of archetypes and number sequences in storytelling[xxxiii] and bring it together with Helga Thoene's analysis of the numerological and archetonal fractal patterns in the final ciaccona of Bach's Partita No. 2 for violin[xxxiv] – an experience beautifully brought to life by the Hilliard Ensemble on their album *Morimur*[xxxv].

The poem then goes on to explore these same patterns in the way life flows through the layers of the earth's ecosystems, weaving these and more into a patchwork quilt of wholeness and on into oneness as the final synthesis.

The poem alludes and references many other equally potent portals which enabled the exquisitely terrifying jolt and contact with the world within and beyond myself creating an ever-expanding and infolding web of reference points of meaning:

I have in the above already referred to, for example, Benoit Mandelbrot's fractal geometry[xxxvi] and Marie-Louise von

Franz's exploration of the origins of numbers, their relationship to time and storytelling, and their symbolic quality beyond mere quantitative instances in her extraordinary work *Number and Time*[xxxvii].

Then there's Psychologist George Hogenson's *Geometry of Wholeness*[xxxviii], a piece which shows corresponding geometric patterns in Western dreams, in Aztec mandalas, and the Chinese I Ching when mapped into Mandelbrot's fractal geometry, the bifurcation graph and the cobweb plot. His work is in turn grounded in C. G. Jung's archetypal depth psychology[xxxix].

These works and their authors explore a journey in and out of chaos and into a kind of life-giving order which is sometimes also called syntropy. Syntropy is the opposite of entropy with which Western culture has a strange fascination. Its concept of time and order are all framed by the narrative that things expire, crumble, wither, and die yet it seldomly if ever reflects on its own role in the process. It is as though even with all the life around us and in us, our fear is so overwhelming that it dictates the way we see the world. So much effort and energy has gone into articulating with greatest precision what entropy is even in the way we tell time; the Western concept of mechanical time is an entirely entropic conception.

As the works referred to above testify, syntropy can also be expressed in great subtlety, detail and precision, for example, in the language of psychology and mathematics which demonstrate the correspondence and meeting place between our inner and our outer worlds.

In fact, one day, without quite knowing what was happening to me, my deep exploration of my inwardness and inner world began connecting to my outer world. What had been meeting me at the intersection of psychology, mathematics, poetry and music began to meet me in the works of ecologists, farmers and health practitioners.

It was the architect and design-theorist Christopher Alexander's *The Order of the World*[xl] which was able to build that bridge for me in greatest certainty. He made the case so emphatically that we cannot only get in touch with the patterns of the natural world through our felt experience of these. We can indeed build on our feeling-connection between our inner and outer worlds and "Make God appear in a field"[xli] as he put it. Like beavers, lions and any other keystone species, we are capable of designing our very own specifically human world within the wider natural world without diminishing or limiting either. We are capable increasing the life-giving possibilities in both when we transcend the either/or perspective and transition into a both/and experience of life.

Alan Savory's work over many decades achieved an articulation of a policy-making framework and management practice which is based on the very understanding that nature functions in wholes patterns. This is in fact the foundational insight of his *Holistic Management*[xlii]. While Holistic Management and its language may on the surface appear closer to military operation than poetry, it actually represents a case of sophisticated left- and right-hemisphere integration which allows the practice to deepen as the outcomes of one's efforts in real life on the land shape the never-ending feedback loop of the human work in nature. Human agency is activated, and work is transformed into conscious action research. (This is as far away as it gets from the mindless carrying out of operational procedures and orders from on high as one can get in the world of work of today.)

There are others such as Pamela Mang and Bill Reed and their work at the Regenesis Institute on regenerative design and development who have helped bring a language to the syntropic possibilities of human interaction with the natural world. In one of their pieces, they quote David Orr on the potential of ecological design: "Ecological design is the careful meshing of human purposes with the larger patterns and flows of the natural world; it is the careful study of those patterns and flows to inform human purposes."[xliii]

Many ecologists, farmers, and food entrepreneurs (who often turn out also to be activists) in their life and work have shown time and again that there is an extraordinary range of possibilities for generative engagement with the natural world that even builds resilient communities and rewards everyone involved financially beyond the wildest dreams of the conventional narrative.

What is going on wherever this kind of situation occurs is that the change in the outer landscape is actually based on a change in the inner landscape which comes before. This may happen in many different ways as the journeys are always, and must always be, unique. However, Ethan Soloviev impressed me deeply with his articulation of the different layers that he has identified in the collectives around us in his work with Gregory Landua in *Levels of Regenerative Agriculture*[xliv]. There is, for example, the great inner leap from the sustainability approach to regeneration which they characterise as the recognition that human beings are part of nature and not separate from it. Ultimately, Soloviev shows a whole spectrum of layers which range from a sense that humans need to compensate for their existence (that is the agenda of the offsetting idea) to the activation of increasingly deeper senses of individual human agency relative to the places in which we can bring our agency to bear and which sustain our existence to a place of co-evolution.

Other examples that have been particularly meaningful for me are Aldo Leopold's explorations of *thinking like a mountain* in his Sand County Almanach[xlv]; Leontino Balbo Jr's journey into and out of being lost during which he experienced the interconnectedness of all things and which led to developing a regenerative-organic approach to sugar cane production which outyields conventional methods by working with Nature[xlvi]; Wendell Berry's revelation that meaningful ecological responsibility is rooted in local knowledge and action, rather than in abstract global policies[xlvii]; Daniel Christian Wahl's work on *Designing Regenerative Cultures*[xlviii] and his notion of health which is more about our capacity to participate than it is about a specific state of the system; and Masanobu Fukuoka's exploration of the limits of human knowing and development of "natural farming" as about "*being* within nature, and living in a way that accords with its cycles"[xlix]; Zach Bush's wide body of work which reframes health and the role of humans on planet Earth as a keystone species also finds itself returning to the human engagement with nature through agriculture as the essential foundation for the alignment for ecological health and human wellbeing[l]; Lyla June's study into the North American indigenous cultures and their regenerative approaches to living in harmony with the land[li] which allowed her to deeply understand the critical distinction between human existence or presence on the planet and the specific social, economic, and political systems that govern human behaviour: by changing these systems—replacing exploitation with stewardship and short-term gain with long-term sustainability—humans can transform from a destructive force to a beneficial one. (She too articulates the possibility of human beings as a keystone species in her work!); and, of course, Robin Wall Kimmerer's beautiful weaving together of indigenous culture, scientific understanding and storytelling in *Braiding Sweetgrass*[lii].

They all tell of a spirit that is sourced from within and which makes for a better world without. This latent possibility in human endeavours since the dawn of time was brought home to me nowhere more so than in David Greaber and David Wengrow's revisitation of the history of humankind in their extraordinary work *The Dawn of Everything* when they write: *"The possibilities for human intervention are far greater than we are inclined to think."*[xliii]

What their work makes clear is that this actually is the norm rather than the exception for human endeavours for much of human history until more recently. It is the indomitable yet joyfully generative spirit that is reflected in works as diverse as Peter Kinglsey's *In the Dark Places of Wisdom*[liv]; Charles Eisenstein's *Sacred Economics*[lv]; Rainer Maria Rilke's poetry[lvi]; Hesiod's *Theogeny*[lvii]; Ovid's *Metamorphosis*[lviii]; Dante's *Divine Comedy*[lix]; Herman Hesse's novels[lx]; Mark Rothko's *Seagram Murals*[lxi]; Anselm Kiefer's *Superstrings, Runes, The Norns, Gordian Knot*[lxii]; Beethoven's 5th Piano Concerto *The Emperor*, E. F. Schumacher's *A Guide for the Perplexed*[lxiii]; Iain McGilchrist's *The Master and His Emissary*[lxiv]; and so many more and what stirs my fellow poet and friend in life, Richard Wain, to write:

Each ecosystem like each heart
Beat out this rhythm from the start
And so it will again my friend
We share a dream.
It's not the end.[lxv]

In the preface to his historical novel, *The Way of Wyrd*, Brian Bates describes how the Anglo-Saxon notion of *wyrd*, in its archaic and original sense, refers to "that aspect of life which is so deep, so all-pervasive and so central to our understanding of ourselves and our world that it is inexpressible. Wyrd refers to our personal destiny. It connects us to all things, thoughts, emotions, events in the cosmos as if through the threads of an enormous, invisible but dynamic web."[lxvi]

This understanding of wyrd originates in Anglo-Saxon culture and recognises fate, destiny, and personal actions as shaping the fabric of existence in a way that emphasizes the interconnectedness of all things. Fate and destiny in the sense of wyrd are not fixed things. The world and the future are not done unto us. Our individual agency matters. While certain aspects of life are governed by *wyrd*, individuals still possess a degree of agency and responsibility in shaping their destinies through their actions. Even though it carries a maybe somewhat sombre tone, reflecting the Anglo-Saxon view of life as precarious and often influenced by forces beyond human control, it also underscores the importance of courage, honour, and resilience in facing one's fate.

As Bates puts it elsewhere, "The pattern of life is not woven ahead of time, like cloth to be worn later as a tunic. Rather, life is woven at the very instant you live it."[lxvii]

Wyrd is a notion that is deeply embedded in Old English literature and its worldview, a telling example of which is the epic poem *Beowulf*. In Seamus Heaney's he writes,

"Often, for undaunted courage, fate spares the man it has not already marked."[lxviii]

Wyrd comes from the Old English verb *weorþan*, meaning *to become* or *to happen*. This is about an ongoing process of becoming or unfolding which emphasises the dynamic and evolving nature of fate.

The Norse counterpart to *wyrd* is *urðr* (anglicized *urd*). *Urðr* (the past) is one of the three Norns of Norse mythology together with *Verðandi* (the present) and *Skuld* (the future). They are personifications of fate. *Urðr* often collectively stands for all three Norns and the web of fate that they weave. This view of the Norns as the weavers of the threads of destiny implies a more structured and somewhat deterministic view of fate than the Anglo-Saxon conception.

In Norse texts such as the *Eddas*, they dwell by the roots of *Yggdrasil*, the *World Tree*, from where they weave their threads into the web of fate which affects gods and men alike.

I hardly have to say it, but just in case, in this rich weave lies the reason for why my poem *Wyrd Awakening* bears its title. The word *wyrd* does not appear in any of the four parts of this long-poem beyond its title, but the whole thing is woven from the same root of the World Tree. We may recognise this weave in the patterns of fractal geometry, in movements of storylines or musical scores, in our dreams, in our biographies or in the patterns of the ecosystems that grant us our lives. *Wyrd Awakening* weaves all of them into the tale of my awakening in this meeting place of my inner and outer worlds.

And now for one final book I must refer to which quite recently led me to experience a most transporting and fertile jolt and the re-discovery of a series of poems I had written in my mid-twenties entitled *Poems from the Global Village*.

Opening my archive box containing these was connected to the portal experience which occurred when I read Tyson Yunkaporta's *Sand Talk: How Indigenous Thinking Can Save the World*.[lxix]

When I re-discovered these poems of mine some 20 years after I had first written them, I found myself reconnecting with something that was essential to me, something of which I was made, and something which I had yet ignored and even rejected.

I am deeply struck by how the themes explored in my writing then have continued to be alive in me in profound ways whilst I had (almost but not quite) forgotten the poems.

There is an obvious and direct connection between now and then, yet things have unfolded in unthinkable and remarkable ways. I am still working on the same things both in my writing and in my outer work with extraordinary, unforeseeable results and vigour. One striking example is the company New Foundation Farms of which I am a co-founder. New Foundation Farms is a food and farming business which is founded on the insight that human beings can be a beneficial keystone species on planet Earth. It is set up as both a for-profit and a for-purpose business and it not only regards economics as part of a healthy functioning of the ecology but recognises that farming, which is normally both an economically marginal activity and one which impacts the ecology negatively, can be significantly profitable when it benefits the ecology. "Food and farming of nature" transcends the scarcity paradox.

But, back to my archive box in which I also found a note by a critic at the time who described the poems as "semi-romantic drivel".

The words hurt. I did not agree. Yet, they had a profound effect on me. Reading the poems back to myself today, I agree with the decision I had taken then to archive them. I was working on some weighty themes, or more accurately put, there were some weighty themes working on me. I just clearly did not (maybe not yet) possess the skill and experience to explore, sort and express them in the way of a writer who writes for an audience of more than just himself.

The feeling then was that, with greater life experience, I may well once be able to do just that. There was no way around this, no short cut, I felt. The way ahead was to live some more and revisit my writing ambitions later. That's at least what I thought then.

It was a tragic and fateful decision which yet carried inside of it the possibility for me to return to the same place once again with greater consciousness, once I was indeed older and at least a more differentiated human being if not a wiser one.

That time is now because it has become clear even to me that the message written to myself and contained within those poems reflects accurately what I have alluded to in the *On Copyright* section of this book:

"Sometimes, writing is like a stepladder into the inwardness of myself. Other times, it feels as though I am being written into being by a poem maybe even over a few decades."

It is worth unpacking this a little more just to show how prophetic and fateful my poems indeed are in my life.

The poem *All the Riches I Inherited* describes me as "a child of the lost race of the city-people that has forgotten how to live." The poem reflects on my intuitive experience of my inheritance of a disconnection from a more authentic, fulfilling way of being alive, passed down from a society that has lost touch with the essence of life itself. Instead of genuinely experiencing life, my observation is that my people are chasing after feelings and states of being, "like happiness, and life, and liberty," that cannot be pursued directly but must be lived to be understood.

The poem reminisces about a time in childhood when, despite being "young and unqualified", there was an innate and quite natural sense of potential for these feelings, "a memory / of an unencountered disposition". This memory serves as a stark contrast to my experience of my reality, marked by a continual search for a place or community where these feelings can be experienced authentically, a place "where I as an individual could live / and in a landscape have a home amongst a people / a place to belong, to connect with others, and to feel human", a place "where I was a human amongst other human beings".

The seemingly endless quest for a place that feels like home only leads to the realization that the escape from one city's confines merely ends in another city's embrace: "roads that leave a city only find another." A perfect cycle of hope and disillusionment.

I realise now that I was then, in my fumbling ways, beginning to put my finger on what I continue to observe about the human condition in modern society where the pursuit of progress and accumulation of possibilities and of material means, paradoxically, leads to a disconnection from what it means to live a truly fulfilling life. Thus, the prospect of real happiness is continuously eroded.

In another one of these poems entitled *The Death of the Human Situation*, the personified human condition of modern urban society completes "what the cities had begun" and jumps from the shadows of the 50th floor of an office tower block to "spread itself amongst the city-people / and sail towards its inevitably silent suicide".

Metaphorically speaking, the human situation undertakes a desperate attempt to escape the confines of its alienation, even if that escape leads to its "inevitably silent suicide": the suicide simply goes unnoticed and thereby reinforces the alienation. This act is both a literal and figurative culmination of the human situation's unbearable pain and longing for release from the dehumanizing aspects of city life. The choice of suicide as an act of spreading "amongst the city-people" represents a final, tragic attempt to connect with the humanity from which the poetic-I of the poem feels so profoundly separated.

Yunkaporta's book *Sand Talk* is the product of a challenging life at the edge of both Aboriginal and Western cultures combined with his innate curiosity and studies which have given him a fluency in Western perspectives on history, systems thinking and particle physics as well as the indigenous knowledge systems of the Australian Aboriginals.

As the book progresses, it develops a framework for looking at and understanding the world through the lens of indigenous knowledge systems, especially Yunkaporta's own Australian Aboriginal perspective. Its focus is particularly on the issues of sustainability, interconnectedness, and the importance of listening to and learning from the Earth's oldest cultures.

From the lens of his indigenous culture, Yunkaporta looks at Western civilisation as an *adolescent culture*[lxx] and offers a critique of its way of being, knowledge systems and approach to life which is as candid and refreshing as it is disturbing.

It was specifically the book's chapter entitled *First Law* which led to the re-embracing of my archived poems. In this chapter, Yunkaporta looks at the crisis of civilisation and the issue of its sustainability from the standpoint of what he calls First Peoples' Law. His prose took me straight to that feeling from which I wrote the poems.

Yunkaporta distinguishes indigenous cultures and First Peoples from civilisations and Second Peoples. The defining characteristic and differentiator of civilisations is that they are "city-building cultures"[lxxi]. Cities, in turn, he defines as "communities that consume everything around them and then themselves." They are the structural difference in the relationship that the cultures of First Peoples and Second Peoples form with the land and wider ecology on which they both rely. The consequence is that city-building cultures of Second Peoples can never be of the indigenous First Peoples kind "until they abandon their city-building culture."

In Yunkaporta's view, city-building cultures rely on an "impossible physics of civilisation" in which foundational laws and phenomena such as time, the second law of thermodynamics and supply-and-demand are distorted and misapplied leading to bizarre concepts such as "sustainable exponential growth."

According to Yunkaporta, this is because "First Peoples and Second Peoples [...] seem to have a fundamental disagreement on the nature of reality and the basic law of existence."[lxxii]

Cities have become divorced from the natural world and yet fundamentally depend on it. This then leads to an outsized negative impact on the natural world beyond its borders: "The biota is stripped, then the topsoil goes, then the water."[lxxiii]

I summarise the chapter in such detail because all of this and the connection to my own poems became available to me in one of those moments I have described as a jolt and portal experience.

Through it, I was able to invite something essential about myself back into my life after rejecting it for two decades.

Twenty years earlier, having archived my writing in a box, I also archived the authentic voice which was speaking through me then. I attempted to banish something of me because it was very painful and by making it disappear, I thought I could avoid the pain. This is a moment of the attempted amputation of the most essential organ described above only to realise that ignoring it did not make it go away. It continued its life in a marginal existence. When I say marginal existence, I mean that it had a full-blown life of its own, only I gave it marginal attention. The less attention I paid, the more painful it became.

I tried to be a good person doing good work along with so many others who are good people doing good work with the best of intentions. But the uncomfortable fact is that being a good person, doing work with good intentions isn't good enough if we actually want to act in service of life and get out of this mess. And we know it. And we feel it. And it haunts us.

Yet, I dedicated myself to arranging myself with the way things are. I tried to find ways to excuse, explain and cushion the status quo.

At this time, although I lived a much more alternative life "in the country", no longer in the city, it was ultimately only a compromise that was still intrinsically measured by what I had described as the life of city people. I had made a big effort, I had moved from urban Germany where I worked in the technology start-up sector to rural England where I then worked for an organic farm. But I had yet to realise that I had taken my cage with me. I, once more, became lifeless and depressed.

Over the years, I learned that trying to say things any other way than I truly feel it, has never enabled me to actually make a difference. It doesn't change things. It has only ever diluted my efforts back into the fold and ways of the city-people. Softening my words to make them more acceptable never actually changed the underlying reality and only offended my authentic sense of self which was smouldering away in the margins from where it curdled my soul. I oscillated between a sense of hope and despair which both have been as disabling as each other, a flash in the pan of my clever mind, expired before it even reached my hands and feet or heart, even if it did inspire a lot of talk and then I'd just go back to sleep.

There was one poem I did not archive. This poem is *My Gallows Star*. I have held this poem dear ever since it formed within the inkblot on the page in front of me as it speaks deeply from within myself even if from within a younger self. Other, more subtle ways of experiencing the same thing have become possible because of it and have led to the long-poem *Wyrd Awakening* as I have mentioned.

I had previously published *My Gallows Star* as part of *Quanticles of Emergence* but that now feels inauthentic just as *Quanticles of Emergence* is Vol. II and not Vol. I of my *Quantum Poetry* as I have given my previously archived selection a life of its own out in the open. And so, I hereby return *My Gallows Star* to its rightful home which feels wholesome and right.

With regard to Vol. II, I feel compelled to briefly comment that this selection of poems came together over some 20 years. The period began more or less with the archiving of *Poems from the Global Village* and ended with my first pilgrimage in Italy to the cathedral of St Francis of Assisi in 2021.

After the pilgrimage, I published this selection of poems as *Quanticles of Emergence – Quantum Poetry Vol. I.*

If you wonder what on earth *quanticles* are, let me shed some moonlight on this wordplay: Just as canticles form a rich and essential part of the Christian liturgy through song and prayer, my quanticles sing of the gospel of the emergence of my inner quantum world and its leaps of consciousness and increasing depth of the experience of being me.

But enough of the talk about poems now. It is time to heed the ancient storyteller's advice – "show, don't tell" – and let the poems show you what they have to say for themselves.

Blessed be the wyrd and introverted and the readers of the patterns of life in all forms from books to landscapes and watersheds, from the meaning of our breaths and actions to the purpose of being human.

May we all meet beyond the *Inkblot Moon.*

ABOUT THE AUTHOR

Marcus Demetrius Link is a creative thinker, writer, and entrepreneurial activist whose work transcends conventional categorisation.

He believes that underneath it all and against the outer evidence to date, there are ways for human beings to become beneficial keystone species. This becomes possible, he says, when we relate in life-giving ways to what we find in those places we call our homes.

Marcus was once dubbed the Quantum Poet during a pilgrimage to the Cathedral of St. Francis of Assisi because of the way he naturally weaves poetic insights across disciplines in search of new perspectives on life.

Beyond his writing, Marcus is a co-founder of New Foundation Farms and of the Holos Earth Project, both examples of radical and practical ventures with a vision of human beings as a keystone species enabled through life-giving ways of being in and seeing the world.

Marcus read philosophy and religious studies at university and is honoured to be a fellow of the Royal Society of Arts.

Born in 1978 on the west coast of Ireland, he grew up in Germany, and now lives in the southwest of England. There, he explores the principles he writes about for real in his life on the land with his partner Clare and their kintsugi[lxxiv] family.

You can find out more about Marcus on his website at foolsjourney.me.

CREDITS

All images and photos used in the artwork of the cover and main body of this book are under license either from *Shutterstock* or *Unsplash*.

I gratefully acknowledge Yingzhao Liu for providing the idea of an ink drop in water to symbolise the possibilities of connection and emergence which influenced the cover design of Quantum Poetry Vol. II, Quanticles of Emergence.

I gratefully acknowledge Tomasz Skowroński's generous permission for the use of his font *zai Olivetti-Underwood Studio 21 Typewriter* which is used throughout this book.

BIBLIOGRAPHY

Alexander C. The Long Path that Leads from the Making of Our World to God. Building Beauty, Sant'Anna Institute, Sorrento, Italy. https://www.buildingbeauty.org/resource-center-entries/2019/8/6/christopher-alexander-the-long-path-that-leads-from-the-making-of-our-world-to-god; 2019. Accessed 27/03/2024.

Alexander, C. The Nature of Order: An Essay on the Art of Building and the Nature of the Universe. Center for Environmental Structure: Berkeley, CA, USA; 2002–2005.

Bach, R. Jonathan Livingston Seagull. London, Turnstone Press; 1974.

Bates B. The Way of Wyrd. Hay House: London, UK; 2004.

Berry W. What Are People For? Essays. Berkeley, CA, Counterpoint Press; 1990.

Brown Dr T. The Philosophy of Masanobu Fukuoka. https://www.permaculturenews.org/2020/07/25/the-philosophy-of-masanobu-fukuoka/; permaculturenews.org; July 2020. Accessed 09/08/2024.

Carstairs K et al. The Rorschach Test at 100. The British Psychological Society. Published at https://www.bps.org.uk/psychologist/rorschach-test-100; published 23/11/2020. Accessed 08/08/2024.

Dante. The Divine Comedy. Translated by Kline AS. Poetry in Translation. https://www.poetryintranslation.com/PITBR/Italian/Danthome.php; published 2000. Accessed 05/08/2024.

De Plessis G & Weathers R. The Integral Jan Smuts. ResearchGate. https://www.researchgate.net/publication/286392418_The_Integral_Jan_Smuts; 2015. Accessed 10/08/2024

Edinger E F. The Mysterium Lectures: A Journey through C.G. Jung's Mysterium Coniunctionis. Toronto, Canada, Inner City Books; 1995.

Eisenstein C. Sacred Economics: Money, Gift and Society in the Age of Transition. North Atlantic Books, USA; 2021.

Ende M. The Never-Ending Story. New York, USA, Penguin Books; 1984.

Fukuoka M. The One-Straw Revolution. New York Review Books Classics; 2009.

Graeber D & Wengrow D. The Dawn of Everything: A New History of Humanity. UK, Allen Lane; 2021.

Grahame K. The Wind in the Willows. London. Methuen Children's Books; 1980.

Hanh T N. The Heart of Understanding: Commentaries on the Prajñaparamita Heart Sutra. Ed. Levitt P. Berkeley, California, USA, Parallax Press; 1988.

Hesse H. Hermann Hesse Facts. NobelPrize.org. Nobel Prize Outreach AB; 2024. https://www.nobelprize.org/prizes/literature/1946/hesse/facts/ Accessed: 09/08/2024

Hesiod. Theogeny. Poetry in Translation. Translated by Kelk C. https://www.poetryintranslation.com/PITBR/Greek/HesiodTheogony.php; published 2000-2002. Accessed 05/08/2024.

Hilliard Ensemble (The) & Poppen C. Morimur. CD ECM New Series 1765, 461895-2. Munich, Germany, ECM Records GmbH; 2001.

Hogenson G B. The geometry of wholeness. In Jung, Deleuze, and the Problematic Whole. Eds: Main R, McMillan C & Henderson D. London, Routledge; 2020. Chapter 5 pp. 125-141.

Jiang B. Living Structure Down to Earth and Up to Heaven: Christopher Alexander. *Urban Science*. 2019; 3(3):96. Published at: https://doi.org/10.3390/urbansci3030096 29/08/2019 . Accessed on: 30/07/2022

June L. Architects of abundance: indigenous regenerative food and land management systems and the excavation of hidden history. A Dissertation Submitted in Partial

Fulfilment of the Requirements for the Degree of Doctor of Philosophy in Indigenous Studies University of Alaska Fairbanks. Published: 12/2022 at http://hdl.handle.net/11122/13122. Accessed: 23/07/2024.

Jung C G. The collected works of C. G. Jung. Vol. I – XX. London, Routledge & Kegan Paul; 1953-1960.

White Cube. Anselm Kiefer: Superstrings, Runes, The Norns, Gordian Knot. Published 2019 at https://www.whitecube.com/gallery-exhibitions/superstrings-runes-the-norns-gordian-knot. Accessed 04/08/2024.

Kingsley P. In the Dark Places of Wisdom. 8th ed. California, The Golden Sufi Centre; 2021.

Leopold A. A Sand County Almanac and Sketches Here and There. Special commemorative issue. Oxford University Press: Oxford; 1989.

Link M. Keystones in the Patterns of Place. Ashburton, Devon, Terranomica; publication planned in early 2025.

Mandelbrot B. The Fractal Geometry of Nature. New York, W. H. Freeman and Company; 1983.

Mang P & Reed B. Regenerative Development and Design. Chapter 303, Encyclopedia Sustainability Science & Technology, 2112.
https://www.researchgate.net/publication/273379786_R

egenerative_Development_and_Design; 2012. Accessed 09/08/2024.

McGilchrist I. The Master and His Emissary: The Divided Brain and the Making of the Western World. New expanded edition. London and New Haven, Yale University Press; 2019.

Morin E. On Complexity. Cresskill: Hampton Press; 2008.

Ovid. The Metamorphoses. Translated by Kline AS. Poetry in Translation. https://www.poetryintranslation.com/PITBR/Latin/Ovhome.php; published 2000. Accessed 05/08/2024.

Rilke RM. *Letters to a Young Poet*. Translated by Kline AS. Poetry in Translation. https://www.poetryintranslation.com/PITBR/German/RilkeLetters.php; published 2021. Accessed 05/08/2024.

Saint-Exupéry A. The Little Prince. London, Mammoth; 2001.

Savory A. Holistic Management: A Commonsense Revolution to Restore Our Environment. 3rd ed. Island Press; 2016.

Schumacher E F. A Guide for the Perplexed. New York, Hagerstown, San Francisco, London, Perennial Library, Harper & Row Publishers; 1979.

Schwartz-Salant N. The mystery of human relationships: Alchemy and the transformation of the self. Hove, Routledge; 1998.

Smuts J C. Holism and Evolution. 3rd ed. London, UK, Macmillan and Co. Limited; 1936.

Soloviev E & Landua G. Levels of Regenerative Agriculture. Terra Genesis International; 2016.

Wahl DC. Designing Regenerative Cultures. Axminster, England: Triarchy Press; revised edition 2022.

Wolfe S. Stories of Iconic Artworks: Mark Rothko's Seagram Murals. Artland Magazine. Published 26/08/2019 at: https://magazine.artland.com/stories-of-iconic-artworks-mark-rothko-seagram-murals/ Accessed: 04/08/2024

Thoene H. A Secret Language – Hidden chorale quotations in J. S. Bach's *Sei Solo A Violino*. In: Hilliard Ensemble (2001). Pp. 47-57.

Tolkien J R R. Tree and Leaf. Smith of Wootton Major. The Homecoming of Beorhtnoth Beorhthelm's son. London, Unwin Paperbacks; 1979.

Von Franz M-L. Number and Time: Reflections Leading toward a Unification of Depth Psychology and Physics. Evanston, USA, Northwestern University Press; 1974.

Wain R. Beyond the Brink is the Beginning. UK, Little Dramas Press; 2023.

Wall Kimmerer R. Braiding Sweetgrass: Indigenous Wisdom, Scientific Knowledge and the Teaching of Plants. Penguin Books, UK, 2020.

Whitman W. Leaves of Grass. London, The New English Library, Signet Classics; 1958.

Wingfield-Hayes G. Farming with Fungi. Permaculture Issue No. 104 Summer 2020 pp. 58-61.

Yunkaporta T. Sand Talk: How Indigenous Thinking Can Save the World. London & Melbourne, The Text Publishing Company; 2022.

NOTES

[i] Morin (2008)

[ii] de Plessis (2015), p. 7

[iii] Smuts (1936)

[iv] Virgil's Aeneid, Book VI, lines 726-727

[v] Link (2025)

[vi] My eternal thanks to Tijs Koonen.

[vii] Schwartz-Salant (1998) p. 18

[viii] McGilchrist (2019)

[ix] McGilchrist (2019) p. xxiv

[x] McGilchrist (2019) p. xxiv

[xi] Schwartz-Salant (1998) p. 222

[xii] Hanh (1988), p. 3

[xiii] Smuts (1936), p. 101-2

[xiv] Smuts (1936), p. x-xi and Chapter V, pp. 84f.

[xv] Alexander (2019)

[xvi] Ibid.

[xvii] Ibid.

[xviii] Schumacher (1979), p. 53

[xix] Edinger (1995), p. 40-43 and 110

[xx] Carstairs (2020)

[xxi] Mandelbrot (1983) and also https://romankogan.net/math/processing_js/mandelbrot.html for a visual impression of the fractal "inkblot" experience.

[xxii] Whitman (1958), p. 72

[xxiii] Grahame (1980), pp.90-94

[xxiv] Ibid., p. 92

[xxv] Ibid., p. 93

[xxvi] Saint-Exupéry (2001), p. 79-87

[xxvii] Bach (1974), p. 51-59

[xxviii] Tolkien (1979), p. 117

[xxix] Ibid., p. 118

[xxx] Ibid., p. 120

[xxxi] Ibid., p. 139

[xxxii] Ende (1984)

[xxxiii] Von Franz (1974)

[xxxiv] Thoene (2001)

[xxxv] Hilliard Ensemble (2001)

[xxxvi] Mandelbrot (1983)

[xxxvii] Von Franz (1974)

[xxxviii] Hogenson (2020)

[xxxix] Jung (1953-1960)

[xl] Alexander (2002-2005)

[xli] Jiang (2019) p. 16

[xlii] Savory (2016)

[xliii] Mang & Reed (2012), p. 10

[xliv] Soloviev & Landua (2016)

[xlv] Leopold (1989), pp. 129-133

[xlvi] Wingfield-Hayes (2020) p.

[xlvii] Berry (1990)

[xlviii] Wahl (2022)

[xlix] Brown (2020) & Fukuoka (2009)

[l] Zach Bush MD has not published many papers and is involved with several projects but there is no book of his own (yet). I have heard him speak on stage and in YouTube interviews. Whilst the website sadly is designed in a way that distracts from his message – at least in my mind –, I highly recommend exploring his work and ideas: https://zachbushmd.com/about/

[li] June (2022)

[lii] Wall Kimmerer (2020)

[liii] Graeber and Wengrow (2021) p. 524

[liv] Kingsley (2021)

[lv] Eisenstein (2021)

[lvi] Rilke (2021)

[lvii] Hesiod (2000)

[lviii] Ovid (2000)

[lix] Dante (2000)

[lx] Hesse (2024)

[lxi] Wolfe (2019)

[lxii] White Cube (2019)

[lxiii] Schumacher (1979)

[lxiv] McGilchrist (2019)

[lxv] Wain (2023), p. 57

[lxvi] Bates (2004), p. ix

[lxvii] Ibid., p. 130

[lxviii] Heaney (2001), p. 39

[lxix] Yunkaporta (2022)

[lxx] Yunkaporta (2022), p. 102

[lxxi] Yunkaporta (2022), p. 57

[lxxii] Yunkaporta (2022), p. 51

[lxxiii] Yunkaporta (2022), p. 58

[lxxiv] Kintsugi (golden joinery) is the Japanese art of repairing broken pottery with lacquer dusted or mixed with powdered gold, silver, or platinum, a method similar to the maki-e technique. As a philosophy, it treats breakage and repair as part of the history of an object, rather than something to disguise. See also: https://traditionalkyoto.com/culture/kintsugi/

Printed in Great Britain
by Amazon

5e19c288-fb6e-4189-bd9d-b7ea5b14b10fR01